3500

CW01642059

The danfo driver in all of us

and other essays

The danfo driver in all of us

and other essays

Niran Adedokun

PRIMA

Copyright © 2019 by Niran Adedokun
The right of Niran Adedokun to be identified as the author of this work has been asserted by him in accordance with the copyright laws.

All rights reserved.

No part of this publication may be reproduced, transmitted, or stored in a retrieval system, in any form or by any means, without permission in writing from the copyright holder.

ISBN: 978-978-56990-1-2

Published in Nigeria in 2019 by Narrative Landscape Press
under it's Prima imprint
9, Odunlami Street, Anthony Village, Lagos, Nigeria
07014522083, 09090554406 – 7
contact@narrativelandscape.com
www.narrativelandscape.com

A catalogue record for this book is available from the National Library of Nigeria.

Cover and Layout Design by Ayebabeledaipre Sokari

Printed by Nutech Print Services

Dedication

To Nigeria, which has remained a dream and to her people; determined but lost in the quest for true freedom. May you attain someday.

Foreword

As a participant-observer in Niran Adedokun's career progression, I feel highly honoured to be asked to write the foreword to this collection of essays ingeniously titled, *The Danfo Driver in All of Us and Other Essays.*

Niran and I, as they say, have come a long way. We were colleagues at *The News* and at *The PUNCH.* I dare say, he distinguished himself at both publications. As soon as I saw the title of this collection of essays, what quickly came to my mind was an article, written in the 90s by that veteran journalist and celebrity editor of his time; Gbolabo Ogunsanwo.

Ogunsanwo, former editor of the *Sunday Times* in its glorious days, had written an article in *The Guardian,* entitled; *The Babangida in All of Us.*

Ibrahim Badamosi Babangida, we will all recall, as military president, was reported to have presided over an administration remarkable for high level corruption. The regime, according to popular account, elevated deception, indiscipline and abuse of office to a high art.

Not a few Nigerians agreed that Ogunsanwo, who now earns a living by preaching the gospel hit the nail on the head. In other words, there is a Babangida in many Nigerians.

Having read through the main essay of this collection from which the author coined the title, I am happy to report (perhaps to Niran's discomfiture), that I don't have a single trait of the danfo driver in me. And, without being immodest, Niran, himself, would testify to that.

The essays addressed contemporary issues in the country; from politics, gender issues, family affairs to entertainment.

Expectedly, Niran brought to bear on his perspectives, the rich experiences he garnered from his days as a journalist with *The News, The PUNCH,* the defunct *Post Express* and *THISDAY*.

For someone with a first degree in Performing Arts and a master's degree in English Literature, it comes as no surprise that his writing is witty and accessible.

This collection of essays from 2014 to 2018, had earlier been published in *The PUNCH, Premium Times, The Cable* and *Facebook*, to mention a few. It is a testimony to the author's passion for change in the country. In the collection, Niran passes the message without being magisterial, thus earning the respect and confidence of the reader.

Let's begin with the title of the collection of essays: *The Danfo Driver in All of Us and Other Essays*. In it, Niran says the Lagos danfo driver is the archetype of the average Nigerian. Attributes of the danfo driver include self-centredness. The average Nigerian, he argues, puts himself first, just like the danfo driver. The average Nigerian, he says, is extremely impatient, ready to circumvent every rule of engagement to gain undue advantage. He, then ended the article with an appeal; "This is a charge to all of us. We owe ourselves the duty of renewal. Let us give our country a fresh opportunity to grow by offering responsible citizenship."

In "Shiite Crisis: Nigeria is Playing with Fire", the author condemns the government's continued refusal to obey court orders to release the Shiite leader, Sheik Ibrahim El-Zakzaky. He then proffers a suggestion; "Would equipping the Police and training its men to respond to those civil issues not save the country from unnecessary bloodletting perpetrated by the military?"

For Niran, there are no "no-go areas" in his areas of commentary. He commented on both the "temporal and the spiritual". The raging issue of the appropriateness of paying tithes in churches did not escape his attention. In "Tithing and the Rest of Us", the author condemned non-Christians who dabbled into the controversy. He, also, didn't spare the Church.

Indeed, he raised a few posers for the Body of Christ: "How is it that every jobless man and woman who can afford a Bible becomes a pastor? How is that there is so much alleged abuse among the clergy and the Church is unable to confront and discourage impostors?"

Niran, also, is an exemplar of the columnist as a prophet. Writing in February 2015, before the presidential elections under the title: "History Will Judge Jonathan and Buhari", he had written: "No matter how the presidential election goes, the history of democracy in Nigeria would not be complete without the names of Jonathan, Buhari and Jega permanently mentioned."

If you remember President Goodluck Jonathan's famous phone call conceding defeat and Attahiru Jega's remarkable calm, in the face of Elder Peter Godsday Orubebe's shenanigan, Niran's prophetic essay comes to the fore.

Niran was equally prescient, in an article written in 2015 titled; "Why the Yoruba May Lose Out under Buhari". The article resonates with the alleged uneasiness of Vice President Yemi Osinbajo in the Presidency.

The author had warned the Yoruba nation about how adept and adroit the North is in deploying political power. He had written; "What the leaders of the North, including the political, traditional and religious are likely to do is to move in on Buhari and shield him from any overbearing influence from any other parts of the country."

Does that remind us of the alleged travails of the Vice President?

Perhaps looking into the crystal ball to predict what might happen four years after, the author noted: "Of course, some would say there is enough consolation in having the Vice Presidency, but between 2003 and 2007, Alhaji Atiku Abubakar, had that office without occupying it. Who says that can't happen again?"

We are reminded that Niran is also a lawyer when we read; "The Futility and Danger of DSS Raid on Judges".

It was the author's opinion that instead of the midnight raid on the residences of judges, including those of the highest court in the land, the government ought to have observed the constitutionally laid down procedures of allowing the National Judicial Council deal with erring judicial officers.

Niran put the president and his aides to the sword when he wrote: "The President and those who serve him, instead of serving the nation, should have known that there could be nothing more corrupt (not even the inducements allegedly received by the judges) than the circumvention of the legal provisions of attaining any purpose in a democracy. Such impurities are precursors to corruption."

In "Soyinka and the Evil that Religion Does", Niran, perhaps for the first time, disagreed publicly with his idol. Soyinka, had advised, rightly in my view, that if religion was not tamed, it could kill Nigeria. But in a well-written and logical riposte, Niran, a devout Christian argued that religion had done Nigeria a lot of good.

But for the religious bodies who provided quality, albeit expensive education, the educational system would have totally collapsed, he stressed. While agreeing that there are multitudes whose faith do not surpass the impulse of their tongues and the pressures of their pockets; Niran asserted that, those we need to tame are "politicians who keep their people poor and ignorant just to use them as canon fodders in the execution of evil plans."

This collection of essays is not all about politics. The author also commented on the softer side of life. In "How Do We Make Better Husbands and Fathers of Men?" Niran related his experience at a forum of single mothers. One of the resource persons had pointed out that "when boys grow up without the mentorship of a man, they are at sea about what it means to be an effective man."

The author who made a name as an entertainment reporter, wrote on the matrimonial feud between celebrity musician, Tiwa Savage and her estranged husband, Tunji Balogun.

He shared the blame equally between the couple. Tunji, he argued, "betrayed the Office of the Husband by going public with those allegations against his wife."

And Tiwa Savage, Niran wrote; "gives the impression of a marriage contracted without much thought. She wasn't even sure whether the union was out of love or fear that age was creeping in and that night might soon fall."

Like his previous book; *Ladies Calling the Shots*, this collection of essays is "unputdownable". This book has depth.

I wholeheartedly recommend it to schools of communication and media studies. Journalists and those interested in creative writing will also find this book useful.

Gbemiga Ogunleye,
Provost,
Nigerian Institute of Journalism,
Lagos

Author's Note

People who know me will testify that I do not have a particularly exciting life. I am one of those people who try to play by the rules – not rocking boats or venturing out of my comfort zone. Even though I practiced as a journalist for nearly one decade, in my career, all I did was cover beats, write reports and effect some quality control on the work of tens of colleagues who were state correspondents across the country. I never imagined that I would write commentaries about anything and gain attention for doing it.

But our lives unfold in parts and every experience leads you to a purpose that we do not immediately see. My stint as Special Assistant to Her Excellency, Toyin Saraki, when her husband, His Excellency, Dr Bukola Saraki, served as governor of Kwara State, brought a deeper appreciation of governance and the essence of citizenship in the development of nations.

These areas have been my focus since I wrote my first piece, which was published in *The PUNCH* newspaper in 2012. It has been six years of great learning about the human condition and the things that make Nigeria a country with so much unrealised potential. I have also discovered that Nigeria's failed dreams are not the real problems; rather, it is our unconcern about our backwardness and the lacklustre efforts to turn things around that are the problems.

From the first day I put my thoughts together in an article and sent it to my friend and former colleague, Emeka Madunagu, then editor of *Saturday Punch,* till today, six years after, working with my dear friend, Joel Nwokeoma, my preoccupation has been to stir Nigerians to play a role in the development of the country regardless of who is elected into office.

The articles in this collection explore issues of governance, citizenship, public institutions, and religion. *The Danfo Driver in All of Us and Other Essays* attempts to deconstruct Nigeria and the people that inhabit it – the proclivities that set us back, the opportunities that we allow go to waste; the potential that we never realise and the future for which we fail to prepare. It is an attempt to motivate us to be better. It is my hope that everyone who reads this book will encounter some transformation that can change our country for good.

Niran Adedokun
September 2019
Lagos

Contents

PART ONE

Of Marriage, that Tiwa and Tunji Spat

In the concluding chapter of his book, *I Married You,* Walter Trobisch, late German marriage counsellor and missionary to Africa, wrote: "Last night, I committed all the errors which I advise other husbands not to commit. I talked only about my work. I told my wife to give a message in church and to prepare another one for the morning. I forgot to kiss her goodnight properly."

On this particular trip to Africa, Trobisch had spoken to members of a community about the ways in which God expected them to treat their spouses and how to make the best of their homes. He spoke about how children should not detract from the attention that the man and woman give to each other and how the one should always put the other's interest ahead. Unfortunately, on that same night, he forgot to do the same thing he preached as he left his wife, Ingrid, to sleep alone and without the attention she craved for, in another room in the same hotel where he was.

Arriving at his wife's room the next morning, he met a broken woman with tears flowing down her cheeks like rain upon a windowpane. Expressing surprise at his wife's early morning testiness, he tried to find out whether it wasn't a good night. The wife complained about how he didn't pay attention to her. He explained that he did not want to disturb her and that he had to write his sermon for the next day. To this, the wife replied: "There you have it; your sermon is more important than anything else."

Trobisch dug in: "But I have to preach on marriage today." Then his wife delivered the death punch. Hear her: "I wonder what you will have to say. You don't understand a woman. You don't know what marriage is. If you only knew how hard it is to be married to you..."

This marriage counsellor who had been married for eighteen years lost his voice for what appeared like an eternity as he realised that even he, had failed in the very thing that he taught people to do. He after all, was as human as any other person he has had to advise on how to make his or her marriage better.

This is one of the reasons why I refrain from the public ecstasy that attends the exposure of conflicts in the homes of other people, especially celebrities. I know for a fact that the most knowledgeable counsellor, if he is blessed to add honestly to his skills, would tell you that there are no marriages without a measure of turbulence. Even in the process of proposing counsel on better ways to manage relationships, marriage counsellors would confess that no two marriages are the same. The situations that people are exposed to and which they have to cope with, are as diverse as the personalities that they have to deal with and so, it is difficult to adopt a one size fits all approach to the issues of marriage and conflicts associated with it.

This is why I find most of the commentaries about the breakdown in the relationship of top Nigerian female singer, Tiwa Savage and her husband Tunji Balogun, unhelpful. In the aftermath of the publicity of Mr Balogun's grievous allegations against his wife, ranging from negligence and infidelity, and the wife's own expose in a video released online, there have been different reactions from condescending to empathetic to dismissal of the couple's right to a disagreement, which is not unusual in a two-year-old marriage. People have made countless parodies out of sound bites from these two celebrities to laugh about.

The question one would be forced to ask however is: "Do you blame the people?" I imagine that reactions to the juicy details about this gentleman and his wife would have been the same irrespective of the nationality of the audience. But this event presents a number of serious issues that can instruct a home whether already consummated or still under contemplation.

I think the man who fired the first salvo betrayed the office of the husband by going public with those allegations against his wife. Forgive my saying it, but I see nothing edifying in a man publicly accusing his wife of being in bed with three or four other men. If it happened at all, I opine that it questions the competence of the fellow's claim to the masculine gender. The nerve to share it, apparently with the intention to diminish the wife, smacks of nothing but immaturity. If he wants to leave his wife because of her unfaithfulness, why doesn't he do it and spare us the lurid details, even for the sake of the child that they have together. Same goes for the attack on his wife's mother, the snide remarks about his own father as well as the drama about committing suicide. People who desire to die do not announce on social media before they take the plunge, this man just made a joke of it all.

And from the apparently contrived response of the madam, she gives the impression of a marriage contracted without much thought. She wasn't even sure whether the union was out of love or fear that age was creeping in, and that night may soon fall. This latter factor is no reason why anyone, especially one who desires a life-long home should marry. Most people who rush into marriage will rush out with the same alacrity. Top on the mind of people who want to marry should be true love (for and from the other person) as well as compatibility. People dismiss the importance of love in a marriage but love actually does accomplish a lot of things, two of which are, selflessness and unending forgiveness without which marriage cannot stand.

People also make the mistake of assuring themselves that they can manage some unacceptable traits in their intended with the hope that they will be able to get that person to change after marriage. The truth is that you are not God, so you cannot change anyone and most often when people change; they change for the worse unless there is some real divinely inspired inner conviction. Prospective couples should therefore advise themselves not to condone behaviours that run contrary to their composition as this is sure to become a sore spot in future.

Over and above, all couples and intending couples should endeavour to commit their relationships into the hands of God. The truth about marriage is that most of it is in the future and only God is omniscient and able to help with that. In addition, every faith has a body of prescriptions that make marriage an enviable and happy institution and most failures come from our refusal to stick with these recommendations. We imagine that we know everything about marriage, but this is a fallacy. Like every other important responsibility that we embark on, there are skills that make marriage work. We must be teachable, ready to learn and adapt every now and then in the matrimonial voyage. It is important that those who marry work together towards a peaceful home in which, if they rear children, these children can grow up in love. It is only when we have homes where children are brought up in love that we can have a peaceful and healthy nation where there is respect for the lives and dignity of others.

In the event that things do not work however, I consider it a duty, which couples owe themselves and their generations, to manage their differences with maturity. This is why marriage is meant for mature people and not children. For the sake of the couple, their children, family and friends, it pays for those whose relationship have broken down irretrievably to part ways amicably and avoid spectacles that may not just make them become foes, but also turn them into objects of ridicule, ruin any chance of reconciliation and affect the psyche of their children and family members forever. For celebrities, those are not moments when you think a journalist is your friend.

The Cable
5 May 2016

What About When Women Abuse Men?

While waiting for our delayed flight to Asaba, the capital of Delta state recently, I joined an ongoing discussion between a group of friends. Emeka Ossai, one of Nigeria's foremost actors and television content producers complained vehemently about the injustice that this world does to men. He contended that there is so much talk about the abuse of women while everyone pretends that men do not go through some measure of even deadlier, abuse. Ossai told his listeners—Fidelis Duker, another Nollywood stalwart; Biodun Kupoluyi, publisher of *E-24 Entertainment Magazine* and Femi Davies of Metronews.ng—that he had already formed a group in response to the silent emasculation men suffer through emotional and psychological abuses from their wives. He then solicited membership from those who agreed with him. Some weeks after this discussion, Ossai said the following in an interview:

A lot of men these days are walking corpses, who due to gross psychological and emotional abuse, have become empty shells waiting to drop. Women have become increasingly aloof in a supposed union with their spouses, while the men have become increasingly powerless to even complain, lest they are labelled as insecure. We are saying enough is enough! I have come across these in people who have confided in me, those I have counselled and some others I have observed. These days you have cases of women beating up their husbands, beheading some, doing bodily harm or wrecking them emotionally with no one in the society reacting. But on the other hand, mere exchange of words with a woman can result to a lot of societal backlash. This is unacceptable! So, under my leadership, we have started a movement of Men Against Spousal Psychological and Emotional Abuse (MASPEA). We intend to sensitise fellow men on this ravaging plight and the society in general to wake up to this new reality. We will encourage abused men to speak up and relate their experiences, engage women of vintage upbringing who do not encourage this trend and are ready to do something about it; and organise counselling for healing and support.

I gave no further thought to this matter until I attended the monthly film screening organised by Goethe Institut Nigeria and the Lagos Film Society.One of the films screened during the two-day event was *Not Right,* a short film on domestic violence, produced by Judith Audu. After watching the ten-minute film, comments were allowed from viewers. While everyone praised the effort put into this debut production by Audu, some men in the audience wondered why no one was talking about the abuse of men.

A gentleman suggested that there was no type of abuse that women go through that men do not experience. He claimed to know several men who were regularly beaten up by their wives and that these men refuse to speak out to avoid the reproach that would most definitely follow. "A lot of men even get raped," he offered as he pleaded that more attention be given to this issue as a lot of men die silently. Now this concern is not peculiar to Nigeria.

There is anger all over the world that campaigners for the rights of people in abusive relationships continue to make the female gender their primary focus. This is true, even though the scanty data available from the Home Office, United Kingdom's statistical bulletin and the British Crime Survey shows that men made up forty per cent of domestic violence victims between 2004 and 2005. This rose to as high as 45.5 per cent in 2007 – 08 but dropped to 37.7 per cent in 2008 – 09.

It would be shocking if an equal, or even higher percentage of Nigerian men do not suffer some form of domestic abuse from their partners, despite our penchant to live in denial. Maybe it is safe to assume that not a lot of women in this part of the world would raise their hands against their husbands, but what about the emotional torture that many men receive? Some researchers in fact believe that that the effects of emotional abuse could be direr than that of physical abuse. This is more so because men are prone to internalising their suffering since society expects them to be stoic, strong and in control.

But some men do get physically abused by their wives, even leading to injury or putting them at risk of injury. This form of abuse could range from physical restraint to pushing, tripping, slapping, hitting, punching, grabbing, shaking or choking the victim. A perfect example is that of the woman who was recently alleged to have sliced off her husband's genitals in Lagos.

Emotional or psychological abuse on the other hand include the use of words, tone, action or lack of action to control, hurt or demean another person. It includes ridicule, intimidation and coercion. I once read an article which quoted published in a book by Smith and Loring in 1994. According to the article:

This man stated that his wife called him ugly, refused to walk next to him in public because she was ashamed to be seen with him, threatened to kill or castrate him while he was sleeping, taught their son to call him "dummy" and "wimp," found the negative in everything he did (including hugging her and buying her flowers), and accused him of having affairs. He felt frightened for his life, blamed himself for everything, and lost 31 pounds…

This story may sound strange to many, but I bet that hundreds of thousands of Nigerian men go through this situation daily. But most men would neither speak up nor move out of the abusive relationship. They are trapped because they suffer a condition known as traumatic bonding, a situation in which the abuser alternates abusive behaviour with kindness, creating a bond that involves intermittent positive reinforcement. This type of bond is difficult to break as it leaves the abused partner hoping that his oppressor would change for good.

However, such a man would likely end up a nervous wreck. The constant abuse would gradually erode his self-esteem and possibly lead him into post-traumatic disorders like you find in women. It could also lead to alcoholism or even behaviours that could be suicidal, self-destructive or self-mutilating, all of which pose a danger to society. Such relationships are also prone to produce children who would grow up thinking that abusing others or being abused is a normal way of life and then subject their own spouses to such abuses or even worse.

Therefore, it is expedient for rights crusaders to begin to consider increasing awareness about the occurrence of the abuse of men and the attendant dangers. In addition to encouraging women to stop the gradual erosion of the dignity of their husbands which may compromise the chance for longevity of his life, campaigners should also encourage men to speak out and seek help before it is too late for them. Society loses out in the long run when men and women cannot play their natural roles because of spousal abuse, this is why the issue must receive timely and comprehensive attention.

The PUNCH
8 August 2014

Are Women Smarter than Men?

Long before I even learned the difference between my left and right arms, I had the impression that women were inferior to men. No one sat me down to teach me about how to disrespect women, but there were things around me that suggested that God meant for women to be subordinate to men.

I have a faint recollection of a story about a situation back in the day. In the environment, where I grew, women who had all girl-children were mostly unfulfilled and depressed. I knew men who kept marrying woman after woman until someone gave them a male child. I knew someone who only stopped after wife number three gave birth to the second girl. By then, he was the father of eight girls from three women, none of whom he wanted to associate with. Women who gave birth to boys walked with pride and were envied by women who were not so "lucky".

The first disappointment I got was in the early days of my primary education. We attended public primary schools in those days where we met people from far and wide. I was top of my class most of the time, which was not surprising because I was the son of a teacher. But when I was not of the top my class, it was a young Ebira girl known as Amina who took the position. Amina, at our tender age, was a pretty girl whose father was a policeman. When it came to academics, Amina was the only one who gave me the fright, and it remained so until we got into Primary Four when she left because of her father's transfer. That experience gave my tender mind a new perspective of the abilities of the female gender. I was sure that my dear friend was going to become someone great. Unfortunately, years later, I would meet her attending to patrons at a petrol station in one of the cities in Nigeria. She lost her father at some point, which disrupted her education as her mum could no longer afford to educate her and her siblings. I left with a heavy heart on the day we met; twenty years after the stiff competition as children. It a sad example of how our society terminates the destinies of promising people.

My early-life encounter with Amina prepared me for the reality that people of the "weaker sex" were neither dimwits nor pushovers, and as I grew older I noticed the way my mother and some of her close friends held their own. In fact, several women in this generation have become single mothers at some point in their lives, and nothing but their strength and smartness could make their children turn out well.

By the time I concluded secondary education, where I met several outstanding girls, I was sure that whoever invented the story about the weakness of women was deluded, at least from the intellectual standpoint. As an undergraduate, I developed more respect for the female gender. Even now, I counsel my male friends not to believe they have stupid sisters, girlfriends or wives—even if the woman chooses to play stupid. Although many men live in the illusion of their unequalled smartness, as I advanced in age, I have come to the conviction that the average woman has learnt to ignore and amuse herself at the superiority complex that a lot of men suffer from. Take infidelity among men for instance. Though most men think they get away with the stupid lies they tell, my opinion is that many women see through those lies and let sleeping dogs lie for the sake of peace. A lot of times, those lies eventually blow up in the faces of men.

On the flip side however, if a woman decides to cheat on her spouse, he would rather be dead and buried before catching her in a lie or discovering the dalliance. Scientists and psychologists have pondered over the differences between the intelligence of men and women for decades. As a result of this, there have been so much varied conclusions to this debate as there have been attempts to unravel the mystery. One thing that most of these researches agree to, however, is that as much as modernity has increased the capacity of all humans to become better at whatever they do, women are moving faster than men.

One study that takes this further and solicits that we surrender our world to women if we are to make progress is by Daniel Amen, an American psychiatrist and New York Times bestselling author. In a study which he described as the "largest brain-imaging analysis ever conducted to evaluate the differences between male and female brains", Amen said his team made stunning discoveries. In an article titled, "Is It Time to Let Women Take the Wheel?" published by *Huffingtonpost* online, Amen explained that, ". . . women showed significantly increased cerebral blood flow in 112 of the 128 regions. . . this means that women generally have more brain activity than men, but what fascinated me as a psychiatrist and brain imaging specialist wasn't that women's brains were much more active than men's.

What I found particularly interesting were the specific areas of the brain that were more active in women—areas that show women may indeed be better equipped to lead our world toward meaningful change than men."

Amen said that the prefrontal cortex—part of the brain also known as the CEO—of women is much more active than that of men. This area of the brain governs things like judgment, forethought, organisation, planning, empathy, impulse control and learning from the mistakes you make, all of which are the "qualities needed to successfully manage a company, lead a nation, mediate crisis, and get people working together towards a common goal."

He explained that increased brain activity allowed women exhibit greater strengths in the areas of empathy, intuition, collaboration, self-control and appropriate worry, all of which are hints of smartness. An article in *The Atlantic* online also recently suggested that companies with female CEOs were outperforming companies with male CEOs by nearly fifty per cent.

American First Lady, Michelle Obama, also joined the smartness debate. While addressing the audience at the US-Africa Leaders' Summit, she joked that "Women are smarter than men and advised women not to 'waste the spotlight'. She said the spotlight is temporary, life is short, and change is needed."

When we discuss that women are smarter than men, can we also apply this premise to the Nigerian woman? Would increasing the opportunities available to women turn the tide of things for Nigeria?

The PUNCH
26 February 2015

Of Runaway Fathers

Penultimate Sunday in church, I heard a story that made my stomach turn. While trying to encourage members of The Fountain of Life Church, Ilupeju, to invite men to Discovery for Men, a quarterly interdenominational gathering of men started by Pastor Taiwo Odukoya in 1997, Mr Taiwo Akinlami, a Lagos-based lawyer and rights activist, noted that this was an extraordinarily difficult time for men and families.

To explicate this point, Akinlami said that the confusion of this season was making a lot of men abandon their homes, either to live with other women or just dropping off the radar without a care for the wife and children at home. He told his listeners that he was privy to many of such cases and he graciously shared one story about a man who left his wife and children and disappeared without a trace. One day, months after he left home, his wife, while driving on the Lekki-Epe Expressway with and the children, saw a man who looked like their erstwhile champion in the company of another woman. They caught up with him at the tollgate; the wife deliberately ran into the car he was driving to get his attention. When he came out of the car and his family accosted him, he flatly denied knowing them. But his accusers did not let him off easy until they were all dragged to a nearby police station.

These are indeed unusual times in Nigeria as this trend is not new, especially in Western countries. An article entitled, "The Extent of Fatherlessness", recently published by the National Centre for Fathering, a United States-based nonprofit, suggests that over twenty million children currently live in homes without a father in the US. The article further indicates that there are millions of other homes where fathers are physically present without any emotional commitments. Another article with the title, "The Nine Devastating Effects of the Absent Father", published last June on thefathercode.com, suggests that about forty per cent of children in the West go to sleep in homes in which their fathers do not live. It adds: "Before they reach the age of eighteen, more than half of our nation's children are likely to spend at least a significant portion of their childhoods living apart from their fathers…"

The point here is that the problem of fathers abandoning their homes is not an entirely new one. I do not even think it is new to Nigeria, although we are not likely to admit this challenge until it attains epidemic proportions and becomes uncontainable. A lane that no society should travel. Even if we do not speak about it, cases like the one cited earlier are on the increase in Nigeria. Every day, you hear mind-boggling tales of men walking out on their families without looking back. You also hear about some who stay at home but have given up their position as husbands and fathers. One of the most common reasons for this is that these men claim to be overwhelmed by family responsibilities. Here, the first thought that comes to mind is the weight of financial demands on the man especially as things get increasingly difficult in this country. As is usual with men, when these financial challenges surface, they do everything to retain their esteem within the family even if it means seeking demeaning jobs.

However, when a man does not communicate his efforts and challenges with his wife, who is also working and dealing with the bulk of the work at home, you find a family that is not walking together and prone to a combustion, which often leads to the ultimate split. Psychologists identify that men who are used to lording it over their wives and children during their financial moments in the sun, are more prone to run away in the event of a turn in their fortunes, which makes it impossible for them to exercise the same level of control. They withdraw into their shells, ready to do anything to save face. This is worse when the family criticizes them about their incapacity, and they run out of their home due to shame and a sense of lack of worth.

But Roland Warren of the National Fatherhood Initiative in the US opines that men who do not feel like the perfect father simply because of their financial state have a gross misunderstanding of the role of a father. According to him: "Good fathers do three things: provide, nurture and guide. Yet, too many men have warped ideas of what this means, and it sets them up for feeling unworthy. The provide part, a lot of times, guys will make that economics. But it's not just about presents… but presence…"

He explains further that some men create a false script of what an ideal father should be and when they don't live up to that wrong image, they feel unworthy and begin to "pull away".

This pulling away is gradually leading to the collapse of the family unit and communal essence of African societies, bringing with it grievous social consequences that we may not immediately see. This is more so because a lot of young Nigerians would now rather just have children out of wedlock than tie themselves to some eternal commitment. This simply means that the idea of children growing up without the attention of a father may soon become commonplace in Nigeria, a signal that portends grave danger for the country.

In the US for instance, some advocates for proper fathering suggest that almost every social ill faced by America's children is related to fatherlessness. These evils, which Nigeria may soon find itself exposed to, include, the rise in the increase of suicide by five times; dramatic increase in the rate of depression and anxiety; thirty-two times average rate of incarceration; lower job security; increased rates of divorce and relationship problems; increase in use and abuse of drug substances; increase in social and mental behavioural issues and ultimate increase in the rate of crime. There is also the problem of decreased education levels and increased dropout rates. Statistics show that seventy-one per cent of high school dropouts are fatherless children, scoring poorly on tests of reading, mathematics and critical-thinking skills. Chances that such children would stay beyond the age of sixteen in school are said to be limited.

When we imagine that most of those who currently misgovern our country came out of functional families and had the opportunity to attend good schools, we should be able to picture the dangers that our country could face with the failure to tackle the increasing rate of the dysfunction of family units. Religious leaders in

Nigeria should now pay attention to the need for families to stay together instead of pursuing selfish pecuniary interests. Just as we need support groups to encourage men and build their capacities to cope with the current economic downturn and whatever interruptions they might face in life.

Most importantly, government at all levels must pay attention to the dwindling ability of the Nigerian to fend for himself and his family. Without concerted efforts at supporting families and respecting government's social contract with the people, the fight against corruption and crimes would remain a joke. But even then, what we see now, is nothing near the impending risk we bear if we do not take care of the family unit.

The PUNCH
29 October 2015

Ese Oruru's Travails: The Shame of a Nation

It was the inimitable Nelson Mandela, who said that "There can be no keener revelation of a society's soul than the way in which it treats its children." Nothing shows the darkness that has gripped the soul of Nigeria and its people like the unfolding story of Ese Oruru, the teenager allegedly abducted from Bayelsa state by a young man who claims to be have been her boyfriend.

This story, which renders like a Hollywood thriller, testifies to the multi-layered descent of our country into shameless insouciance – an appalling state in which no one but ourselves and people, or things, that concern us matter. Sadly, this selfish, "me, I and mine" tendency is invariably causal of most of the ills that holds our country back.

On 12 August 2015, Mrs Rose Oruru, a food vendor in Opolo, Yenagoa Local Government Area of Bayelsa state, came back to her shop to find out that her thirteen-year-old daughter was missing. After hours of trying to trace the daughter, she got hint that a long-standing customer of hers named Yinusa, also known as Yellow, had abducted the girl and taken her to Kano to convert her to Islam to enable him to marry her. Yinusa, apparently a Kano native, was a commercial tricycle driver until that day when he, by the account of his kinsmen, sold his vehicle, ostensibly to ease their journey.

Two days later, the distressed mother set out for Kano in the company of one Rabiu who allegedly took her to the chief of a village in the Tufa area of the state. The chief, angry at Rabiu's audacity for leading the distraught woman to him, flatly told Mrs Oruru that her daughter had converted to Islam and could not be said to belong to her any longer. To add steel to his claim, the chief was said to have invoked the name of the Emir of Kano, Sanusi Lamido Sanusi saying to them that the girl was now in his custody.

Cut the story short, this woman and her family travelled between Bayelsa and Kano states on a number of occasions without even having as much as a one-minute physical access to their daughter. During these trips, there was abundant evidence that the matter had been brought to the attention of the Emir of Kano and his council, the Assistant Inspector General of Police (AIG) Zone1, Commissioners of Police in Kano and Bayelsa states among many others but the girl remained in the custody of her abductors until a ***Sunday Punch*** story lifted the veil off the conspiracy.

Soon after the report, Sanusi's palace issued a statement denying ever having the girl in custody. Sanusi also said that he had instructed the Kano state Shariah Commission to liaise with the AIG Zone 1 to assist in taking her back to her parents. But the question to ask the Emir whose statement seems more of an attempt to guard his reputation than alleviate the plight of the abused girl and her parents is, would his response have been the same if she were his daughter?

That is if we discountenance the information from a police source that: "The Emir said that since she voluntarily said she wanted to be a Muslim and had converted to Islam, her parents should not force her, and that even though she is a minor, she should be allowed to practice whatever she wanted to practice. It was the girl that followed the man; she was not taken by force..."

If we take no cognisance of the foregoing because it came from an unnamed lowly police officer, what about this information from the Inspector General of Police, Mr Solomon Arase: "The Emir decided that he was going to mediate. But, because of his trip to Mecca with the President; that was what caused the delay. But now that he is back, we are going to sort it out as quickly as possible." The Emir clearly invested more interest on this matter than he was willing to concede, but that is by the way.

The real tragedy is the denigration of the office of the chief law enforcer of the land by no other person than its occupier. That Arase, a lawyer, would share the above sentiment with a newsman shows that he sees nothing wrong in subjugating the authority expressly provided his office by the 1999 constitution to the monarch. It is telling of the extent to which institutions in Nigeria are pliable to the pleasure of the high and mighty. But the degradation of the police goes further. Why would the police in a country bound by laws including in this case, the criminal or penal code (depending on where the case is being tried) and the Child Rights Law adopted by many states allow this matter to get to its highest echelon before culprits are prosecuted? Nothing tells more of the hopeless state of national institutions.

In a society where institutions perform without prompting, where loyalty is to the state and not cluster interests, the intelligence and police authorities would have handled this issue without drawing national attention or whipping ethnic and religious sentiments capable of further weakening the structure of the society. A police force which arrests and detains citizens on civil matters, which is prone to being illegally employed to enforce contracts suddenly becomes toothless, requiring the support, endorsement or approval of the powerful emirate before obeying the law breaks the hearts of the people who sustain it. So, in the unlikely event that the Emir is found on the wrong side of the law, how does a fawning agency respond?

The most tepid of all nevertheless, is the duplicity inherent in our collective sense of catharsis when stories like that of Miss Oruru hit the news when we are privy to similar incidents on a daily basis and do nothing about them. Millions of Nigerian children are out on the streets, denied of care but state governments who now issue preachments look on. This is why even Yinusa would have been a water fetcher, tricycle rider and God-knows-what-else in his short eighteen years.

Girls are forced into marriages, raped and exposed to inhuman conditions on a daily basis in this country. Yet, we look the other way until our child or relative is involved. An account actually suggested that Ese Oruru was not the first girl to be abducted in the area. But for the courage of the parents, we would never realise that girls get the Chibok girls' treatment across the country. How do we sleep when the fruits of the future are abused, plucked forcefully before they are ripe? Would a society which gives its children no education, no protection, ultimately not breed brigands and at best, misguided adults?

This case, even if it appears so, is not of the Romeo and a Juliet stock. It is laden with the manipulation of an impressionable mind teased by the promise of affluence. For instance, one is forced to query where the SUV Ese was sighted in Kano came from when her abductor was a mere commercial tricycle operator in Bayelsa.

Ese Oruru's travails tell of the failure of the state and federal governments to protect citizens, it is an eloquent narration of the pervasive roles of poverty and ignorance in our search for national identity. It tells of our impenitence as a people and shows that this nation is not working for a future in which the bulk of its children can be global citizens. It shows we have lost our soul as a nation and it demonstrates the urgent need to find our soul again.

The PUNCH
3 May 2016

How Parents Can Save Nigeria

In the 1987/88 academic session, I sat for the Interim Joint Matriculation Board (IJMB) Advanced Level Examinations. When the results of the examinations, which came after two years of intensive coursework at the Kwara state Polytechnic Ilorin, were released, I failed Geography, one of the three mandatory subjects that I took. History and English Literature, the other subjects I entered for, gave me a meagre five out of the possible fifteen points, hence I could not get into a university. My father, then in the Kwara state Civil Service, refused to intervene on my behalf. He told anyone who asked him to speak to people he knew at the university that he would not go begging on account of his son's unimpressive result. I lost the academic year.

From that experience, I learnt two invaluable lessons on success. First: There would never be an adequate excuse for laziness and lack of preparation. Second: Failure is an opportunity to do things better. And for these two lessons, I have my dad to thank. If he had forced my way into the university with those poor results, I would have taken everything for granted and possibly gone ahead to make a mess of the undeserved university admission. I could tell endless stories of how parents insisted that their children walk the moral, even if torturous, way in my childhood.

This is the lesson that many parents today fail to inculcate in their children. The average parent is in pathological fright of failure, yet he does not encourage hard work as an antidote to failure. All we teach our children these days is the importance of being successful and wealthy, without much care about how success and wealth are attained. We forget that the health and sustenance of society is more dependent on the values of hard work and respect for procedure than ostentation of success and wealth.

A friend related this heart-rending story to me. On the day that candidates were writing Economics in the current General Certificate of Education (GCE) organised by the West African Examination Council (WAEC), he had taken his ward to one of the exam centres in Lagos. There, he noticed that certain candidates brought mercenaries into the venue after supervising officials were "settled". According to him, the real candidate and his hireling would write the examinations at the same time although in different rooms. After the exams, invigilators replaced each candidate's answer sheets with that of the mercenary and destroyed the former. This story explains some of the strange aftermath of secondary education in the country. It explains why students make excellent results in WAEC/GCE without the intellectual capacity to pursue university or polytechnic education. It would also account for Nigeria's recent notoriety to produce unemployable graduates.

The tragedy of the situation is the involvement of parents, even community leaders in this "must-pass-examinations-and-get-into-highe institutions" mentality that has gripped our country. While there is nothing wrong in aspiring that our children get the best of education possible, we put the future of the country at risk when we manipulate the ways of students who do not qualify to get into these institutions. Here is how: these students would likely meander their way through higher institutions and thereafter unleash their half-baked, mediocre aptitude on the society. Having mastered the art of manipulation, they are the teachers, doctors, lawyers, engineers, accountants, bankers, politicians, pastors and imams of Nigeria's future. One thing is certain: The future of a country where almost everyone is a con artist is bleak.

These ill-tutored young people will not just ruin Nigeria, they will also be unable to compete with their mates from more serious countries. Now, smaller countries like Ghana are doing better in the education of their children than the giant of Africa. How do we then compare ourselves with countries like China where students go as far as tying their hair (with clothespins or scarves) to ceilings in an effort not to fall asleep while studying? The idea is that every time they nod off, the pins will pull on their hair, jerking them awake. How do our own laid back, indulged youths compete with such hardworking children in the future?

Currently, government at all levels in Nigeria concern themselves with the building of infrastructure while the moral firmament of the country is tattered. Of course, the building of infrastructure is laudable, but it is only a matter of time that children who do not understand the value of hard work will destroy whatever physical structure that we build today. While the elites train their children in private schools across the world, they forget that society is organic and that these well-trained children would be at the mercy of those who remain at home sometime in the future.

Government needs to take an emphatic and serious look at restructuring education in Nigeria. We must lay emphasis on fitting the right pegs into the right holes. For instance, attention needs to be paid to the quality of teachers produced in the country. The students that are admitted into many Teacher Training Colleges (TTCs) are those who could neither make it into universities or polytechnics as the cut-off marks into TTCs are lower than that of other institutions. Hence, they draw the not-so-good, not-so-passionate, bottom of the rung students of education who then go on to become teachers. As no one can give what they do not have, it is important that the foundation—the quality of education teachers get—is solid because that is the first step to transforming the education space.

Over and above everything, this country must begin to embrace the virtues of hard work and diligence once again. Countries that achieve greatness live by a moral code to which everyone - ruler and ruled - are subject. Unless this happens, everyone - wealthy or otherwise - risk a country which might come crashing on all our heads.

The PUNCH
20 September 2014

Again, Nigeria Swallows Fifty Children

How could a country lose more than fifty defenceless innocent children and move on so easily? A suicide bomber marched into Government Comprehensive School, Potiskum, pretending to be one of the students but only being on a mission to kill and maim. Primed for maximum effect, the bomber detonated the explosives while students were on the assembly ground. At the end of the confusion that followed the explosion, mangled bodies littered the ground; maimed children shrieked in pain and darkness filled many a future so bright. Thus, began and ended another Monday of sorrow, tears and blood in the world's most populous black nation.

The next day, the first citizen stormed the nation's premium open-air events centre, the Eagle Square in Abuja, to declare his intention to run for a second term in office come February 2015—three months down the lane. His supporters said there was nothing wrong with the president's declaration. They argue that the date was already fixed. They also say that incidents bothering on massive loss of lives were becoming too frequent with occasions in which the president had already planned public events. The incidents appear orchestrated, and it would send wrong signals to the evil doers if the president were to give in to the manipulation of the enemies of the nation.

It would be unreasonable to say that they have no point, so I sympathise with them. I also ask: what would have happened if the president delayed the declaration just for the sake of those innocent children, making the point clear to everyone, including the perceived perpetrators of those evil events? These children whose lives were snuffed out at dawn, sought nothing more than a bright future, from which the country would benefit. And they deserve a last respect from us.

As a matter of fact, how would sparing us the spectacle of that declaration have impacted negatively on the chances of the president in the elections? However, more than all of this, the real issue is the failure of Jonathan's presidency to mobilise Nigerians of all shades of opinion to stand behind him in defence of the nation against these criminals.

It however did not go down without the opposition kicking Jonathan. Candidly, I would have been worried if on the day after Jonathan's declaration, I did not read any statement from National Publicity Secretary of the All Progressive Congress (APC), Alhaji Lai Mohammed describing the event as "mindless", "insensitive" and "callous".

However, the loss of these innocent souls did not stop the "APC northern caucus and some elders from the North" from meeting on the possibility of having a consensus presidential candidate on the same Tuesday that Jonathan declared, according to media reports. The only difference is that this was done out of the view of discerning Nigerians.

By Wednesday morning, the APC thought it was fair time to celebrate with Governor Adams Oshiomole on the sixth anniversary of his administration. There was hardly any significant name in the APC that did not partake in this elaborate event in Benin, just 48 hours after the massive loss.

So how are our leaders able to move on despite the wanton loss of innocent lives in the country? How do politicians divorce themselves from the pervading sense of foreboding hanging over us all? What does the way they move on after the loss of lives, especially of innocent children, tell about our humanity as a people?

The Nigerian political elite has failed the people. While we have resigned and accepted the wastage of national resources on their insatiable appetites, the failure to fight the real war is dangerous to our national survival. The real war is to protect the future represented by these children who are daily killed and maimed in an irrational war entrenched by the failure of government to deploy its coercive power to guarantee public safety.

From the testimony of Governor Ibrahim Gaidam of Yobe state, Monday's attack was the fifth on schools in the state in a little over twelve months. Previous attacks were on the Government Secondary School, Damaturu where eleven students were reported to have been killed on 16 June 2013; Government Secondary School, Mamudo, where thirty-three students were killed on 6 July 2013; College of Agriculture, Gujba, where seventy-eight students were reportedly killed in September; Federal Government College, Buni-Yadi, where fifty-nine children were reportedly killed on 24 February 2014 and now, Government Comprehensive School, Potiskum, where about fifty children were murdered on Monday.

So, in seventeen months, Yobe state has lost about two hundred and fifty school children to this insurgency. No one is keeping the records in Adamawa, where over forty students of the Adamawa state University, Federal Polytechnic and School of Health Technology, Mubi were said to have been killed on 1 October 2014. Add that to over two hundred girls kidnapped from Government Secondary School, Chibok. This should make us all turn in our beds with worry at night.

Yet our leaders carry on like all is well when several questions remain unanswered: why do state governors keep schools, which are very soft targets open? Why have they not provided adequate security for these schools? Why do they only offer medicine after death—shutting them down after havoc has been wreaked? Why are we not thinking of alternative ways to provide education in such danger-prone zones?

Given the burden of educational disadvantage that the North-East in particular currently suffers, it would sound counterproductive to suggest the closure of all schools in the region until such a time when it becomes manifestly safe, but wouldn't we rather have these children alive? In any case, it would take years of planning and conscientious execution of that plan to reverse the existing educational disadvantage in that region.

Authorities in the region appear contended with preserving the status quo than engendering change. For example, there were pictures of the Borno state Governor, Kashim Shettima handing over Naira notes to some children. Although there was no explanation for the images, the action came across as the opposite of what a leader, concerned about the future of those children would encourage.

The Federal Government talks about a Safe School Initiative for the North-East, which involves governments of the states, but if it is taking too long for this initiative to take off, states must find creative ways for these children could get educated without so much risks to their lives, otherwise, they should shut down the schools until their safety can be guaranteed.

Nigeria's ruling class does not realise that the way children are treated is a measure of our society's humanity. Nigeria owes them protection from avoidable dangers and the opportunity to attain the best that life can offer. Without that, we would be nation without a soul. And the political class should make no mistake about it, unless every child gets a fair head start in life, they would be exposing their own children, who they spare nothing to nurture, to a future even more monstrous than what Boko Haram currently presents. The time for that harmonised development plan for the states in the North suggested by Governor Mukhtar Yero of Kaduna state is now.

The PUNCH
14 November 2014

Who Needs a Gender Equality Law?

Truth be told, I am done nerve-racking about Nigerian politicians. As it is, nothing will make those who play politics in Nigeria put the interest of the common man above their personal, class and party interests. At least, not until the common man himself realises the muscle in his own democratic rights and flexes same to his own advantage.

This is why my new-found source of concern is the ordinary Nigerian. I worry that we cry over small potatoes while the big ones rot. We sleep on our rights and allow politicians lead us anywhere and anyhow. We follow them without a whimper, like flock led to the slaughter. I worry that unless we wake up to the reality of our responsibilities as citizens, this country goes nowhere.

This is the sense I came away with when I read about the rejection of the bill on gender and equal opportunities proposed by Senator Abiodun Olujimi, representing Ekiti South. I was shocked by the quality and quantity of interest that the failed proposition generated. I still do not understand the hoopla about the law and the response of the Senate to it.

To start with, how the rejection of the law shocked Nigerians when within the two weeks preceding, we had ample tokens of the disposition of two prominent senators. Dino Melaye, easily the most outspoken member of the 8th Senate, had two weeks earlier, derogatorily talked about women like they were pieces of items to be purchased from a shelf when he was talking about patronising Nigeria-made goods.

A week after, Majority Leader of the Senate, Ali Ndume suggested that the only way the senate could help women was via multiple conjugal associations. To him, the ultimate misfortune of a woman is not having a husband and since so many of them are approaching menopausal junctures, it was better for men, whose capacity for nurturing the unfortunate is endless, to double their portion. That done, our women will not only feel accomplished in this world, they will also have automatic tickets into eternity, on account of the marriage they contracted while living, seems to be the Bornu Senator's thinking.

In this same senate is a man who, not too long ago, flew across Africa to woo a thirteen-year-old and has unashamedly continued to defend the right of such children to be married. God knows how many men of his conviction warm the seats of the senate. It then beats imagination that Nigerians expected people of such disposition to support anything likely to deter their amorous proclivity for a moment. How could we be so naïve?

But away from that, how many of us actually realise that even if the National Assembly had a second reading and goes on to pass the bill into law, it may only have effect in the Federal Capital Territory?

Someone would say that a passage by the National Assembly would make it possible for states to adopt the law, and I agree. But what if the states refuse to adopt the law? What if they adopt it and do not implement it? Before you imagine that this is impossible, ask about the Child Rights Act, domesticated and passed into law by the National Assembly in 2003. This Act prescribes a life sentence for anyone who has carnal knowledge of a child, whether female or male and fourteen years imprisonment for other forms of sexual misconducts. Today, thirteen years after the Act was signed into law by former President Olusegun Obasanjo, only twenty-four of our thirty-six states have domesticated the law. And most of the twenty-four states are at various ineffectual states of implementation, with many of them watering down the definition of crimes and punishments for them.

But then again, why exactly do we need that law? On the broad issue of discrimination and equality in Nigeria, the 1999 Constitution (as amended), which is the supreme law of the land, is emphatic about the rights of all citizens and any law inconsistent with the constitution cannot stand. Also, several other laws in Nigeria address some of the issues that I imagine this law would attempt to address, but do we put them to test? For instance, adultery is a criminal offence in some parts of Nigeria, so is bigamy under the Marriage Act. Also, just before he left office in May 2015, former President Goodluck Jonathan signed the Violence Against Persons Prohibition (VAPP) Act 2015 into law. This law, among other things, prohibits female genital mutilation, forceful ejection from home and harmful widowhood practices. It also prohibits the abandonment of spouses, children and other dependents (without sustenance), battery and harmful traditional practices.

So how many short-changed women have come forward to explore opportunities that the Marriage Act, the Criminal Code, the Penal Code and a number of such other legislations provide? Don't we always find some emotional or cultural reasons why a woman cannot file an action against her husband and father of her children? What new thing do we hope to achieve with this law that the senate gave us a song to sing about last week? Will the law initiate actions against those that flout it by itself?

Nigerians need to prove that these laws work and send offenders to jail. Let prominent women, who understand their rights encourage women who have no idea to explore the laws and stop suffering in silence. I confess to not being conversant with the provisions of Mrs Olujimi's proposition but if there is indeed any substance to it, Nigerian women should be mobilised to fight for the law and demand its passage.

Nigerian men and women of good will should insist on the adoption and implementation of the Child Rights Act by all states in the federation. I consider education to the best first step towards liberating any society. Women who have the benefit of education know what to do when men trample on their rights and every man, worthy of the nomenclature, knows how to accord women respect and give them their due. Curiously, many of such men sit in these same chambers where you have these rabid paedophiles.

If all states adopted and implemented the Child Rights Act, without tampering with the definition of the age of a child, Nigeria would have all its children in school and growing with the self-confidence that makes them hold their own in future.

Most importantly, we need to begin to interrogate repugnant cultural, traditional and religious practices which are against natural justice. A lot of the things that hamper the expression of women in Nigeria are more cultural than legal, and until we fight these cultural tendencies to a standstill, its custodians will stand in the way of pro-women laws.

Women should desist from being apologetic about asking for an improvement in their condition because closing the gender gap and giving women equal opportunities is actually an important catalyst to economic productivity and improved development outcomes. And limiting such opportunities will deprive Nigeria of a better future.

The PUNCH
24 March 2016

Is It Really a Woman's World?

Not too long ago, I had a discussion with some female friends who asserted that it was a woman's world and that men just live in it. Their argument made sense in a way. These were ladies who have never lacked anything in their lives. They came from what you would call privileged backgrounds. They did not know what it meant for a father to refuse to send a girl-child to school because the family could not afford to pay the fees of all its children, and since a girl would get married and take another man's name, she could as well make the sacrifice for her male sibling. It was opportunity cost, simple.

These friends of mine grew up seeing their fathers pander to every desire of their mothers. They were ferried to school out of Nigeria very early and never experienced the deprivations that girls suffer when they manage to make it to school. They grew up surrounded by drivers, stewards, nannies and bodyguards. In the very unlikely event of a car ever breaking down, the driver broke the sweat or at worst, they called dad, or brother or boyfriend or lately, husband to come and deal with it while they hopped on the next taxi home, even unable to wait for another driver to pick them up.

Marriage to a woman like this is nothing more than a contract or business relationship. If it works, so be it, if not, what the heck. There are no eternal sacrifices. The guy would not dare raise his hands against them and they never worry about infidelities or any other kind of misbehaviour. "Let him just try it," they would say, assuring you that he would pay heavily for it in such a way that he possibly would never recover.

So how do you blame these kind of people when they say that the world belongs to them? They live in a world which is oblivious of the travails that poor sisters all over the world suffer. They are insulated from the stories of millions of girl-children who are out of school all over the world. They are unfamiliar with twelve-year-old Malala Yousafzai, who was shot and left for dead by Pakistani extremists for daring to speak up for education. They do not hear of girls, barely out of diapers who are forced into marriage. They do not know about women who have suffered untold consequences from philandering husbands, women who have lost their lives from the physical, emotional and psychological abuses from men. They do not know about diseases that ravage women because of forced marriage or the risks that hundreds of thousands of women are exposed to just because they get pregnant and are about to bring children forth. They do not seek employment from anyone neither are they interested in politics and so they are unaware of the reality of the glass ceiling or the discrimination that limit the aspirations of women. They are just in a world of their own and cannot empathise with women who are not in luck as they are.

But in the real world where you and I live, life is much harder for the female gender. Dosomething.com, a United States of America based not-for-profit platform for young people and social change, quoting Amnesty, gives some statistics that we should consider. An article titled "11 Facts about Women around the World" states that one woman dies from pregnancy or childbirth every ninety seconds in the world, with about eighty per cent of these preventable deaths, mostly in developing countries The report also indicates that violence against women increases during pregnancy and that women make up eighty per cent of refugees and displaced people all over the world. This is as a result imply that instruments of genocide such as sexual violence and rape are often directed at women and girls. The report shocks further: women make about fifty per cent of the global population, yet they fill less than twenty per cent of parliamentary seats all over the world. Even more shocking is the fact that women account for seventy per cent of the global population living on less than one dollar a day. So, how then can it be a woman's world?

In Nigeria, things are no easier for the female gender: Fathers confess to raping their children, mothers are subject to domestic violence, widows are raped by boys as young as their grandchildren. Daily, newspapers are filled with sad tales of how women are demeaned, their humanity subdued.

So, the question remains: how do we change this narrative? Women need to be empowered through access to quality education. For instance, what is Nigeria doing to make girls knowledgeable family planners, competent mothers, more productive and better paid workers, informed citizens, confident individuals and skilful decision makers?

Between sixty and seventy per cent of the forty-six million illiterate adults in Nigeria are believed to be women. And of the 10.5 million children who are said to be out of school in Nigeria, it is believed that not less than sixty per cent are girls. How this would improve in the very near future is totally uncertain especially given that most of the girls who are currently out of school in Nigeria are from the northern part of the country where the Boko Haram insurgency and child marriage make any educational revolution unlikely.

Former United States Secretary of States, Hillary Clinton wrote in her preface to "Global Women's Issues: Women in the World Today" that not giving women, equal opportunities to grow "...offends our basic sense of justice and fairness. But it is unacceptable for another reason too – because it keeps countries from making real progress in creating jobs, sparking economic growth and giving all their people an opportunity to create a better future. No country can advance when half its population is left behind. In short, women around the world sustain families, build communities and knit the social fabric together."

For any country to attain its potentials in today's world, all hands, whether they belong to men or to women, must be on deck and Nigeria cannot be an exception.

The PUNCH
7 March 2014

How Do We Make Better Husbands and Fathers of Men?

I had the privilege of being amid a group of women who came together to find communal succour, even if fleeting, from the strains of their circumstances–single motherhood.

The stories of these ladies were as diverse as their shapes and sizes. Those who lost their spouses to the cold hands of death were few; there were some who left their homes after many years of being unfulfilled, and there were others who returned home one day to find their husbands had walked out on them, never to return. All the ladies at the meeting, convened by Deola Erogunaiye-Olulana's initiative "Precious and Pretty Moms" at the Energy Academy, G.R.A, Ikeja, had children. It was a touching event.

A particular lady decided to leave her matrimonial home after she had suffered from physical and emotional abuse for about twelve years, because she would "rather be alive as a single mother and take care of her children alone than be dead". Another lady, slim, gorgeous in her ebony skin, emotionally spoke of how she had been "beaten and battered" for five years without anyone, not even her parents, knowing. He left her and their two girls two years ago, and she is happy taking care of her two beautiful girls.

The other painful part of their situation is the stigma attached to being a single mother. There was a consensus that some women choose this status, but they are well-heeled, without any care about what society feels. On the other hand, those who single motherhood is foisted on them, ironically, do not get our sympathy. With the likely exception of widows, whose challenges are even more enormous albeit of a different dimension, women who become single mothers say they are treated like pariahs. One common example is the alleged discrimination from landlords who not only insist on having their husbands with them before giving out their homes, but make snide comments linking their status with prostitution or promiscuity.

Then the guest speaker for the evening, Mrs Betty Irabor, Editor-In-Chief and Chief Executive Officer of *Genevieve* magazine, relived her own compelling, almost fifty-year-old story. She started with something like: "I thought I was coming to speak to you about how to find strength but listening to many of you speak, I am the one that has drawn strength from you." Irabor told the story of how she and her siblings were raised by her mum. However, she did not know why her mum left her marriage, at some point leaving them with their policeman father.

"I remember my dad doted on us, at least for a while. And then, one day, I went to school with my younger brother, I was about eight or so. As we were coming in, I noticed that a truck was parked in front of our home at the barracks and I recognised some of the things in the police truck. I was wondering who was packing our things. Then, my father came out with two paper bags. He walked to us and handed over those bags to us. I discovered that one had my things and the other had my brother's things. That was the last I would see of my father for over twenty years." Irabor said to an attentive audience wrapped in the stun of an incredible story.

She had no idea where her mother stayed and had to depend on compassionate neighbours who traced their mum and handed them over to her after explaining the shocking departure of their father from home. Irabor related with the challenges of single mothers, still living in the freshness of her own deprivations which hurt so much that she refused to see her dad when he appeared at her doorsteps over twenty years later!

Although it was a gathering to encourage single mothers to pick up the pieces of their lives and be strong for their children, I left with a strong sense that unless something is done about the upbringing of men, we will continue to have stories like the ones these ladies shared. As Deji Irawo, one of the resource persons at the event pointed out, when boys grow up without the mentorship of a man, they are at sea about what it means to be an effective man. It can then safely be said that the failure at building the capacity of boys to becoming responsible men either because their fathers are not there to mentor them or that their fathers were themselves not properly taught, accounts for the increasing number of men who are unable to cope with the complexities of modern-day relationships.

In addition to so many others, there are three specific roles that fathers plays in the lives of their children. The first is that a father confers identity on his children. He also confers the sense of self-worth on his children, giving them a sense of belonging and history, which every child needs. Lastly, the father is the one who gives children a sense of validation. He is the first coach and mentor of the child; the child's biggest fan and encourager. It does not matter if the child is male or female, the father is the one who builds confidence in a child from a position of acceptance and love in a non-judgmental environment which helps the child interface with life. Children who do not find this level of devotion from a father will certainly seek their identities, validation and sense of worth from elsewhere, and this is at the root of antisocial behaviour that plague societies. It is the absence of anyone to impart such capacity in boys that make them develop without the ability to deal with the realities of man/woman relationships.

For instance, the basic instinct of the average male child in this part of the world is to see himself as superior to the woman. He takes this sentiment to his relationship with the opposite sex and gets married without the mental capacity to cope with a woman who can hold her own. He becomes defensive and gets violent.

One of the services "Precious and Pretty Moms" hopes to offer its members is mentorship of children by several men who have offered to work with the group. The idea is that to stop the vicious circle of male abandonment and irresponsibility, children with single mothers should get occasional father figures who will prepare them for the emotional and psychological demands of manhood and save our country from men who bring violence home and eventually abandon them.

The PUNCH
14 July 2016

Death, Now Two for a Kobo in Nigeria

Sometime in the 1970s, the Juju music maestro, then known as Chief Commander Ebenezer Obey, did a track wherein a line lamented the cheapness of death in the country. The line "iku di meji epinni," meaning "death has become two for a penny", spoke about the frequency with which people, especially young ones died. It talked about the low life expectancy in the country and waxed spiritual by wondering whether this was a result of sin. Were he still in his elements today, one can only imagine what the great music composer and musical artiste would be singing.

At the time Obey released this music, those who died, even if they were young, died mostly from natural causes, largely due to the evolving state of medical sciences, not just in Nigeria but across the world. The state of medicine has since improved so much that illnesses, which killed people in the 1970s, have either been totally eradicated or healthcare delivery has improved to prolong the lives of people or save them from such ailments. But not Nigeria. The world seems to have moved on and left our dear nation behind.

Although Nigeria is significant for her population and large mass, it is notorious for supplying the world with the worst developmental index possible. A 2015 report of the National Population Commission suggests that a total of fifty-two thousand people die annually from childbirth or pregnancy related complications. In other words, one woman dies every ten minutes in the process of bringing a new life, and the World Health Organisation says at least 70% of these deaths can be prevented if women had more access to skilled medical care. Medical science has found solutions to complications like post-partum hemorrhaging (excessive bleeding); hypertensive disorders (eclampsia), prolonged labour and infections that account for the preponderance of incidences of mortalities resulting from pregnancy. But not Nigeria.

In addition to the number of corpses of women of childbearing age that Nigeria piles up every year, 2300 children under five years old die from a myriad of causes that the country is still grappling with. World Health Organisation (WHO) says that an average of 240 Nigerians die from cancer every day in Nigeria. This translates to ten people every hour and a total of 80,0000 in a year. Nigeria is said to introduce an extra 100,000 cases of cancer into the world's burden annually, yet the country has less than one radiotherapy machine per one million people; hence, the Nigerian cancer death ratio of four out of five cases. At least 300,000 fall into the cold arms of the grim reaper through malaria every year not to talk of the number of lives lost to non-communicable diseases and other infections that most of the world no longer contends with.

Sadly, it is clear that no one, leader or led, pays attention to the tragedy of healthcare delivery and what the unquantifiable volume of lives lost does to the image and future of Nigeria. Government at all levels, of course pays lip service, voting billions of naira to the sector annually, but there is no manifest improvement in access and quality of healthcare delivery from the primary, secondary and tertiary levels in Nigeria, which is a shame.

But the failure of governance and the humanity of Nigeria is even more evident in the unbridled level of cold bloodletting that happens in the name of ethnic/religious clashes and other violent crimes. The country just seems to have been taken over by some merchants of death. It is so bad that Governor Abdul'aziz Yari of Zamfara state recently raised the alarm about his inability to maintain law and order in his state. This was after thirty lives were lost in one week. A report published in *THISDAY* newspaper in May 2018 suggested that nine hundred people were killed in such violent circumstances in the first five months of 2018. This included Benue, Taraba, Kaduna, Kwara, Plateau, Nasarawa, Niger, Kogi and Adamawa states.

Then another two hundred lives or more were added to the list when three local governments in Plateau state came under the attack of herdsmen who were said to be avenging the killing of their kinsmen as well as the theft of their cattle. What happened that Sunday of the incident was not new though. Time and time again herdsmen have wrecked this inhuman havoc on helpless communities, which have been justified as their reprisal to the violence the Fulani herdsmen have experienced in the past. It is more curious because, as we have seen in the case of an incident in Jos, the Miyetti Allah Cattle Breeders Association of Nigeria, the umbrella body of the Fulani herdsmen, justified these events, and even the presidency helped to ventilate it. For instance, the statement released by the presidency on that Sunday quoted security information that indicated that about one hundred cattle were rustled by a community in Plateau state, and some herdsmen were killed in the process.

It also shows the incompetence if not complicity of law enforcements agencies in the country. If security forces, who had the statement issued by Senior Special Assistant to the President on Media and Publicity, Malam Garba Shehu, knew that cattle had already been rustled, then they should have ensured that the owners of the cattle got justice by arresting those who perpetrated the crime and deploying resources to forestall further reprisals. That none of these happened should mortify the security forces and stop them from making excuses of the initial crime. This excuse by the president's spokesperson only portrays the nation's security apparatus as reactive and inefficient. But, more importantly, it reflects the total disrespect for life amongst us as a people. Over the past couple of months, government officials including the minister of defence has exposed the lack of will to deal with this situation with suggestions that states that have enacted laws to protect their people against the incursion of Fulani herdsmen may have to repeal those laws before there can be peace in the country. What the powers that be fail to realise is that such postures unwittingly embolden the citizens capacity to seek self-revenge and invariably wittingly down the essence of the country's law ultimately turning the country into barbaric state in which power is might and reasoning are lost.

There is no sane society where a man can take the life of another without consequence and even if that happens, the state takes the offence as one done against it and not against the receiver of the aggression. Without this, the world would live in disorder and lives, even of those who are innocent of any crime, would be in jeopardy. The gradual degeneration of Nigeria into a killing field is the failure of government to hold the lives of citizens with the sanctity that it deserves. And when government shows no respect for lives, the people follow suit. This is why there is so much bloodletting around us; if it is not Boko Haram, it is the Fulani herdsmen or ethnic militias or armed robbers, kidnappers or even frustrated policemen who turn their guns on innocent citizens. Death just seems to lurk in corners across the country.

But Nigeria's only redemption from the current path of self-destruction is for its people to place more of value on the lives of the people who make the country. No country, where death is so commonplace can truly aspire for greatness. No matter how much resources it has or how much infrastructure it builds, human life is the essence of society and a single human life should be worth more than all the treasures that man can acquire. Nigeria needs to re-learn that.

The PUNCH
28 June 2018

Finality of Death and the Lessons Men Fail to Learn

I was fascinated by the dramatic form, tragedy, from the first day I was introduced to it. Arthur Miller, one of the most renown theorists on the subject, says, while dismissing the perception that tragedy was synonymous with pessimism in a February 1949 essay titled, "Tragedy and the Common Man" that "…in truth, tragedy implies more optimism in its author than does comedy, and that its final result ought to be the reinforcement of the onlooker's brightest opinions of the human animal. For, if it is true to say that, in essence, the tragic hero is intent upon claiming his whole due as a personality, and if this struggle must be total and without reservation, then it automatically demonstrates the indestructible will of man to achieve his humanity…"

Although there are basic disparities in the perception of the Grecian tragic hero as propounded in Aristotle's *Poetics* and Arthur Miller in this essay, there is a convergence of understanding concerning the emotions that tragedy evokes in the writer and the audience alike. Aristotle talks about the evocation of fear and pity (pathos), which leads to a purgation of emotions or what is called catharsis. Miller does not contradict that. He insists though that the common man is as suited as the noble for tragic heroism, but all men know fear, all men can pity a man who falls from grace to grass as a result of a character flaw or in the pursuit of meaning for his life. All men can feel emotional purgation from and relate with such happenstances.

I always imagine that this is the emotional state that the death of loved ones should leave man. Although death, without the elements listed amongst others, is not within the conception of tragedy from the point of view of dramatic theorists, the transition of people from this world should always remind of the temporal nature of life and cause men to seek God and the good of others. This has been my state of mind since the passage of my father-in law, Comrade Sam Isichei, within twelve hours of the onset of a sudden illness. His death, shocking and paralysing, again brought the lack of empathy amongst Nigerians, especially some medical personnel. When he fell unconscious the night before he passed on, he was rushed to a medical facility. We were told that the personnel at the hospital vowed not to touch him until a deposit was made and they did not. When money was eventually brought, the doctor commenced treatment by administering some intravenous medication and disappeared until about 9 a.m. the next day. His patient lost the battle of life not too long after. Maybe, the doctor saw that the situation was bad. Maybe, that knowledge inspired his lackadaisical attitude, but then, who knows what prompt medical intervention could have done. Sadly, such promptness is alien in the vocabulary of many Nigerian medics. Where they stand, money is superior to life and unless you hold money, your life could as well hang in the balance. But this is not just about doctors; it is pretty much a national attitude.

Even more intriguing is our hypocrisy. Despite our failure or refusal to intervene when we could have saved lives, we become expert mourners when it is too late. However, we only mourn those who are alive. Like the tragic hero in a work of art, he who is dead is out of the battle; fighting the good fight is left for the living. Because we forget that one day, fire will burn without the man who roasts yam with it, we eat the yam that belongs to us without consideration for others and if they are unwary, we appropriate their own out of avarice. The suspension of contemplation for the reality of the end is why we have the wicked endless plundering which had plunged tens of millions of our compatriots into hunger, disease and lack. Were men a bit more conscious of the transience of life, they would be less motivated by personal proclivities and a bit more considerate of others.

Someone said that life is not how long but how well. But how well you live it is a function of the number of lives you touch positively. The people that you touch and the impact you make on the world are the things that people, and eternity will remember about you. But do we pay attention? These thoughts have been on my mind in the past three weeks of the sudden passage of this great man. Isichei and I did not get along well for a while. When his daughter announced her plan to marry a Yoruba man, he would have none of it. For close to four years, he maintained his stance, defying his brothers, sisters and friends who saw our commitment and thought we would be good together. But his daughter and I were resolute about what we wanted, and God helped us to wait out his objection.

Interestingly, I sympathised with him. I saw that his concern was for the wellbeing of his daughter. This man was no ethnic bigot. He grew up in the North and spoke Hausa like a native speaker. When we eventually got married, he encouraged me to learn Igbo as he encouraged his daughter to learn to speak Yoruba. He was a true nationalist in his corner. At our wedding, he danced like his life depended on it. He became a father to both of us. He displayed no entitlement, but generously blessed us with stuff we didn't have access to. He taught us about contentment and encouraged us to work towards our goals. He was good with his grandchildren; he would sing with them on the phone, clap with them and encourage them to be the best at everything they could lay their hands on. He was a very happy man. It was impossible for Isichei to join a company and not leave an impression. He lit up everywhere he went and had compassion for people. Even in retirement, we saw the activism that once led him to the office of the vice chairman of the Nigeria Labour Congress in Delta state. He was principled and suffered no fools. He and his wife raised their only daughter to be a woman who made them proud as a wife, mother and professional. He was a blessing to this world. And suddenly he left us, without the benefit of a warning.

His passage is the single most effective sermon that I have listened to recently. From the time his youngest brother, Dr Chris Isichei, who monitored events on the phone, broke the news of his death that Friday morning, I had wondered how pleasant the world would be if men took the lessons of their mortality a little bit more seriously. What would happen if men became more truthful in their service to God and love for humanity, wouldn't the world be devoid of man-inflicted pains and sorrow? What if those who appropriate our commonwealth remember that they cannot take any of it with them at death? What would happen if people who profess God think more about the prospects of heaven and hell and those who do not, consider what posterity would say of them? How much better would Nigeria be if (wo) men realised the worth of a good name, if they thought of the interminable end that death brings.

These are the things that have occupied my mind since the man joined the saints triumphant. In my musing, I realise that life is about those who are living and the lessons they draw from the lives of departed ones. May we find the grace to live life well.

The PUNCH
15 September 2016

Curbing Maternal Deaths in Nigeria

Every year, thousands of medical practitioners, policymakers, development workers and advocates for improved healthcare delivery for women converge for the ***Women Deliver*** Conference – a global conference organised by Women Deliver, an advocacy group comprising a coalition of organisations working towards generating "political commitment and resource investments to reduce maternal mortality and achieve universal access to reproductive health."

The conference prides itself as a platform which brings together voices from around the world to call for action against maternal death. It builds on commitments, partnerships, and networks mobilised to achieve Millennium Development Goal 5, which is the reduction of the maternal mortality ratio by three quarters. As expected, tens of Nigerians will be at the conference. The Health Minister will travel with a retinue of colleagues from the Federal Ministry of Health and its parastatals. They will join the ministerial forum at the conference reeling out loads of statistics on efforts being made to arrest maternal mortality and morbidity in Nigeria. As government representatives show the world that progress is being made, Nigerian charities pontificate on their efforts to change the "death" narrative.

I do not begrudge any of them. They have a right to show the world what they are contributing to the movement towards improving maternal health in Nigeria. What bothers me is that things are not seriously changing. In their three days at that conference for instance, about 426 Nigerian women may have died from childbirth or pregnancy-related complications. And that is no exaggeration at all. Statistics show that a woman dies every ten minutes from childbirth and pregnancy. Official figures from the National Population Commission claim that there are 52,000 cases of maternal death in Nigeria annually. This would amount to about 142 deaths daily. The report also hints that for every dead woman, there are twenty cases of morbidities such as obstetric fistula, infections and disabilities. More recently, the Society of Gynaecology and Obstetrics of Nigeria was quoted as saying that an average of forty-five women died from pregnancy complications every day between January and March this year. Any death resulting from pregnancy, childbirth or within 42 days after delivery would be considered as maternal mortality.

It is not likely that any of these figures is anywhere near correct. Nigeria currently has no standard way of recording anything. The records brandished at various levels are without doubt from those of women who presented at hospitals, at hospitals where proper records are kept for that matter. The hospitals where these records come from are also very likely, mostly in the urban areas, in places where women realise the importance of prompt and adequate medical attention during pregnancy. It is possible to contend that far more women die unrecorded in the rural areas in Nigeria. The reasons are not farfetched. There are fewer healthcare facilities in the rural areas. There are even fewer women who go to these few health care centres for reasons that include lack of access, finance, and sometimes, ignorance.

The situation in Nigeria is more depressing because the World Health Organisation (WHO) and other partners working in this area have identified that about eighty per cent of the total maternal deaths recorded in the world are preventable and prevention only takes simple conscientious planning and multi-level collaboration in the case of Nigeria.

By far the most worrisome cause of these mortalities is lack of access to skilled medical care. There are too few primary healthcare facilities, and when they are available, they are sometimes too far away for easy access, especially in emergencies. This brings up the problem of transportation. While the WHO recommends that a woman visits the hospital at least four times during pregnancy, hundreds of thousands of women in this country, do not receive any form of medical attention until they fall into labour, even then some do not go to hospitals. When some women then fall into labour or encounter pregnancy complications only timely, skilled medical intervention can guarantee any chance of survival. And when that is not available, the life of the woman and sometimes that of the unborn child would be at risk.

Asides the many challenges that bedevil the medical sector, another reason why there are inaccurate records of maternal deaths is the tendency for people to easily resign to fate—or "let us leave it to God syndrome"—when they lose lost ones. This lack of accountability favours a struggling medical sector. It however, denies the nation any opportunity to track that mortality, learn from it and prevent another one. This worsens the national condition, as it constantly becomes impossible to identify and address the most important demands for the survival of women, it makes planning impossible.

These challenges show that addressing the unacceptable number of maternal deaths in the country means improving access to medical health as well as providing skilled medical personnel. Dealing with the former is not just about building and equipping hospitals, it must involve dealing with the problem of ignorance, which is largely fuelled by traditional and culture practices that stop women from attending ante-natal clinics and planning their families.

To address this, government must involve traditional, community and religious leaders, showing them the benefit of these simple medical practices to the survival of women and children. It actually would not be out of place to wield the big stick on any erring party after massive awareness campaigns.

In 2010, the Kwara state Government introduced a law which was initiated in the state House of Assembly by Mrs Toyin Saraki's "The WellBeing Foundation". Among other things including making medical care free for pregnant women and children under-five all over the state, the law also provides punishments for men who ban their wives from hospitals during pregnancy. Ondo state is also making progress in this area. This kind of law is needed in every state, especially in the Northern part of the country where maternal mortality is alarming.

On the issue of skilled medical personnel, it is important that government at all levels embark on the recruitment of well-trained personnel. There was the Midwives Service Scheme—a programme in which the three tiers of government collaborated to get retired midwives back into service to fill the personnel gap – introduced by the National Primary Health Care Development Agency (NPHCDA), But as it is with Nigeria, that laudable programme only lasted for a while.

The National Health Council should consider a large-scale response to the maternal and child mortality challenge as we did with HIV/AIDS. The response to the HIV/AIDS scourge included the setting up of action committees at the federal, state and local government levels. These committees are made up of people from every possible sector of the Nigerian economy and this has contributed to the success that have been recorded in stemming the rate of new infections, reducing stigmatisation and arresting the loss of lives.

The rate of maternal, newborn and child mortality in Nigeria is currently at an emergency proportion. The world is at a point at which every nation serious about development must move decisively. Even if Nigeria cannot meet the MDG 4 and 5 in three years' time, the country must set and work towards new achievable targets. A nation which allows her women to die in the process of bringing forth lives only exists on borrowed time.

Premium Times
4 May 2013

PART TWO

Soyinka and the Evil That Religion Does

Nobel laureate, Prof Wole Soyinka, is what his Yoruba people of South-West Nigeria describe as "Akanda". I do not know an English word that captures the import of this word, but if we attempt a translation, it would mean someone specially created by God without duplication. This is how I have always seen Soyinka and here is why. Before he became a significant literary figure in his late twenties, Soyinka had set himself on the path of influence when he, alongside six other friends, set up the Pyrates Confraternity at the University College, Ibadan.

Even if there has been an irredeemable adulteration of the original idea, this was arguably the first hint to the anti-establishment disposition that would reflect in all of Soyinka's endeavours till date. Today, what he created at the age of eighteen has reared a colony of loyalists committed to the ideals and who are willing to go any length for the first ever "Capone". You probably have also read about a young man who once hijacked a radio station at gunpoint to protest what he believed was the rape of the people's will. Such deliberate activism, without consideration for his personal peril, marks the life of Soyinka, even now in his eighties.

In the literary ecosphere where he stands out like light in darkness, Soyinka has built a cluster of devotees.

Consider the fluidity with which he swings among the three genres of literature. Recall the elegance and rhythm of each quatrain in the poem, *Abiku*; the anger, humour and sarcasm of *Telephone Conversation*; the prophetic audacity of *A Dance in The Forest* and the intense probe of the psychology and nature of man in *A Man Died*. It is impossible to encounter Soyinka's life and depart without an indelible impression. If you are not taken by the brilliance of his art, you will be awed by his dexterity with the English Language, or by his courage and activism. In fact, I have always opined that but for education and the liberation that it brings to the souls of men, we would one day behold the deification and worship of Soyinka! I agree that is rather hyperbolic but ponder this: in the past couple of years, I have identified many points of disagreement with Prof Soyinka. What is curious however is that I have never expressed the disagreements publicly. Why? The reason is that I idolise Soyinka. What I think the English describes as "hero-worship". I think many Nigerians are confined in enclaves such that many public commentators refuse to see, hear and speak evil about this great man. This disposition is peculiar to people like Soyinka whom Nigerians do not fully understand; therefore, they cannot intelligibly interrogate him. This was the sense I got from his recent counsel on the need to tame religion, which could kill Nigeria. While we can concede that Soyinka referred to the death of Nigeria only figuratively, it presents an opportunity to impeach suggestions that religion is guilty of the troubles that has plagued our country.

Indeed, on the contrary, I propose that religion has indeed done this country better than it has been credited with. I will give a few examples of that. Take education. While public education has been ruined by successive governments in Nigeria, that we still have a semblance of quality education today is to the credit of these religions. At all educational levels, religious bodies have established schools where they nurture children and prepare them for the future, which the state would have denied them. People will present arguments about how these schools are expensive, but they are at least available to save us from the costlier repercussions of ignorance. They save us from the venom that an angry, uneducated generation would vent on an uncaring country in future.

Their interventions include providing medical treatments and the stabilising effects that good family units have on a country that as thrown morality to the dogs. Speaking about morality, make no mistake, those who have true convictions about the God maintain the fabric of morality on which this country stands. And there are so many who will not dip their hands into depravity on account of their adoration for the Almighty. Without these ones, Nigeria would be a far sorrier state than our current lamentation. No doubt, there are multitudes whose faith does not surpass the impulse of their tongues and the pressures of their pockets, those who employ religion for the attainment of selfish, ungodly and anti-people goals, pretty much the same way in which we have people employ traditional African beliefs for antisocial reasons. But even these take a cue from the recurring plague that we call leadership. This latter group and their sponsors are those that we, as a people must tame.

Nigeria needs to tame people of Soyinka's generation who, having sucked the best of the milk that the breasts of this country produced are now too terrified to speak to power. I wonder for instance, how a country with seven of its former leaders alive would allow the Boko Haram situation escalate to this level. This is considering the fact that five of these leaders, hail from the Northern part of the country and that this terrible phenomenon never started on the plate of religion.

Those we need to tame are politicians who keep their people poor and ignorant just so to use them as cannon fodders in the execution of evil plans. Those we need to call out are ethnic lords who imagine that they own Nigeria and strive to subject everyone to their authority. Come to think of it, are these violent acts actually always borne out of religion? The recent unfortunate attacks on Southern Kaduna did not have their foundation in religion. It is a continuation of the conquest exploits of a group of people afflicted with a superiority complex. It just so happens that the marauding army and their victims happen to find themselves on different sides of the religious divide.

You can go further to cross-examine the attempt to tar religion with this violent brush by asking why those of us who come from other parts of the country do not turn guns on our cousins and nephews who adhere to diverse faith. In the family in which I was born in Kwara state, I lived with Muslim cousins with whom we went to church and ate Sallah meat. In this same family, we had a section which celebrated the Orisa-oko festival every new yam season. We all played a part in it without disagreement let alone violence. Religion, by itself is therefore not Nigeria's problem. Those we need to watch out for are the misguided ones, overreaching themselves, drunk on false doctrines, exuberance and pretentions. These ones and the people who back them up with the powers of state are those whose wings need to be clipped by Nigerians of goodwill.

The PUNCH
19 January 2017

Where Are the Youths to Lead Nigeria?

There is a debate at the National Assembly and among everyone who imagines that Nigerian youth have consistently been denied access to high political office.

You may have encountered some politicians alluding, shortly after independence, that the future belongs to the youths and how those same politicians are still piloting national affairs fifty-five years on. Since return to democracy sixteen years ago for instance, Nigeria has, at various times, been at the mercy of one sexagenarian and a septuagenarian. Both, taking a second shot at the slot.

The first, chief Olusegun Obasanjo was negotiated back to office by fellows of his gerontocratic communion from around the country. He became the civilian presidency at the age of sixty-three, relinquishing power to his choice of successor when he turned seventy-one. Obasanjo ruled Nigeria with the authority of an African patriarch, whose word is law and command is decree. With him in power, the people's desire for a younger leader grew like a deer panting for water. And by some happenstance, since Obasanjo is not exactly popular for deferring to public opinion, he was succeeded by a much younger man who was succeeded by another younger man.

Unfortunately, by the end of the administration of President Goodluck Jonathan, majority of Nigerians were ready to try the leadership of anyone irrespective of age. In response to some remarks about the age of then presidential candidate, Muhammadu Buhari, his supporters drew parallels from the triad of South Africa's Nelson Mandela, America's Ronald Regan and Britain's Winston Churchill to justify electing someone in the autumn of his years as president. With unusual passion and near unanimity, Nigeria sought a Buhari presidency, hinging this desire on his legendary integrity, an aptitude, which was long lost in our leadership.

Even then, many Nigerians insisted that the country deserved a younger leader. One year into the Buhari administration, members of the National Assembly are considering legislating this into fruition. Hon Tony Nwulu, a People's Democratic Party (PDP) member representing Oshodi/Isolo Federal Constituency II, recently proposed a bill seeking to alter Sections 65, 106, 131 and 177 of 1999 constitution as amended. This is to reduce the age qualification for the offices of president, governor and senator from forty to thirty years and twenty-five years respectively in order to open public offices to younger people and expand the age bracket for political participation. Nwulu made copious references to jurisdictions like the United Kingdom, France, Norway and several countries in Western societies where the age qualification for political participation is much younger. He spoke about the need for Nigeria to expand the frontiers of democracy and quality of political office holders by considering lowering the barrier of entry.

I imagine that advocates of young people into active politics would hail this gesture, which has already passed second reading and may soon become law depending on the successful amendment of the constitution, but I consider this to be one of those impulsive steps that Nigeria leaders take in total indifference to our realities. Such leaders will always run themselves and society into socio-political quicksand. While it is true that the situation of the Nigerian youth has progressively deteriorated over the years due to policy failures, entrenched self-interests and incompetence on the part of successive leaders who have undermined the competitive capacity of our society, to imagine that lowering the age qualification for nomination to high political offices would solve this problem is indicative of lack of rigorous contemplation.

The first question to ask proponents of this amendment is what happens to the academic and intellectual capacities of the individuals who aspire to these offices? Do we still leave the basic qualification at school certificate?

Secondly, do these lawmakers realise that a chunk of our youths is still struggling to get out of higher institutions due to admission delays and incessant strike actions inflicted on them while on campuses at about ages twenty-five and thirty? And those who are out are still searching for a steady means of livelihood, jumping from one danfo bus unto a commercial motorcycle, resume in hand, in search of increasingly diminishing employment opportunities. Do we want to surrender political office to people who would see politics as meal tickets?

The only other possibility is that these offices will be passed on to offspring of politicians and upper-class Nigerians who attain academic qualification at relatively young ages. In which case, we would be excluding the majority of Nigerian youth, handing over political offices to the children of the same people who have destroyed the country. Were our law makers not too removed from reality, they would realise that the fundamental needs of young people are a working society where functional education is available and affordable, where attaining gainful employment is not herculean, where security is assured and prosperity flourishes. They would work for a society where no one is discriminated against on account of age, sex, religion or tribe. A nation where individuals with industry, intellect and ingenuity can actualise and build castles of prosperity without affiliations to Daura, Bourdillion, Otuoke or Ilorin. When we erect such pillars of shared prosperity, young people will not need the generous solicitation of law makers before demanding their rightful place in the organogram of power in a society in which they are an integral part. And this does not have to be in politics.

Professor Wole Soyinka, who would later go on to win the Nobel Prize for literature, wrote his first major play, *The Swamp Dwellers* at twenty-four. This was followed by the hugely successful *Lion and the Jewel* one year later and the oracular *Dance of The Forest* in 1960 when he was twenty-six. Same goes for Professor Chinua Achebe, whose magnum opus, *Things Fall Apart,* was accomplished at twenty-eight. Professor Iya Abubakar had worked as a visiting professor at the University of Michigan before his thirtieth birthday. He was later appointed as Professor of Mathematics at the Ahmadu Bello University (ABU).

Same can be said of some First Republic politicians. Chief Obafemi Awolowo's book *Path to Nigerian Freedom* was published in 1946 when he was freshly called to bar. He set up the Egbe Omo Oduduwa one year later in his late thirties. At age thirty, Dr Nnamdi Azikwe had become a household name in most of Africa, while Sirs Ahmadu Bello and Abubakar Tafawa Balewa formed the Northern People Congress (NPC) in their thirties.

Although we still argue over the auspiciousness of the Biafran war, that secession attempt was led by thirty-four-year old Lt Col Odumegwu Ojukwu who prosecuted the war with philosophical sophistication. His opposite on the Nigerian side, General Yakubu Gowon became head of state at thirty-two. Now, just a few of these men had any privilege neither did they attain these posts for being young. They were qualified and flourished in a society that gave them the best.

The law reducing the qualification for political participation is therefore, at best self-serving. It gives its proponents away as agents of the materialistic school of politics where access to power is equal to flinging the door open for younger people to plunder the commonwealth. Were their view of politics in conformity with Jeremy Bentham's utilitarian school where power is an avenue for service and seeking the happiness of the greatest number of the people, they will focus on fundamental, progressive and futuristic appreciation of energies of the younger generation than the tradition of allotment that currently defines our politics.

Dynamic laws are required in education, culture, sports, science, law, innovation and entrepreneurship all with the potential to jump start Nigeria into a position of respect within the global community and inspire faith.

We should create an open society that encourages a culture of debate over political fraternity that has crippled our leadership selection process. But this age reduction initiative is a knee-jerk initiative, which is not able to lead Nigerian youth to any better future.

The PUNCH
21 July 2016

The Big Business of Kidnapping

The morning I heard about the abduction of Toyin Nwosu, wife of Steve, Deputy Managing Director of Sun Newspapers remains one of the most petrifying of my life. Toyin and her husband, both of whom I have been friends for about fifteen years, are easily one of the most lovable couples the world would ever have the benefit of and I could not imagine what would make anyone contemplate something injurious to this wonderful family.

For the first hour of being privy to this worrisome news, I stood numb in one position. Strains of worry gripped me, and I could not find the will to do anything—not even stand. I picked my phone, but I could not call anyone, not any of our mutual friends. I abhorred the prospects that anyone would confirm the story. I dreaded mentioning it to my wife and my brother and friend Toni, with whom I ordinarily share such things. I wanted to stay in disbelief forever and did not want to be the herald of such untoward news. When I would eventually tell Toni after about ninety minutes of grappling with my confusion, his first question was "have you called Steve?" I told him I could not imagine the trauma a man being asked to confirm his wife's abduction would be passing through and if the event that the story was true, he would definitely be in no position for calls like mine. The call that the man would expect most at such a period, would be one from the abductors or security personnel. After talking for a while, I agreed that I would call Steve.

Two hours later, I did. Someone picked the phone.I think it was Steve but the low tone with which he spoke told me the whole story. I hung up, looked up to God and said a simple prayer of faith that God should kindly seek out this our precious Toyin and bring her back unhurt.

One of the reasons why it was difficult to come to terms with Toyin Nwosu's abduction is that her husband did not have bags of money anywhere. And of course, people get kidnapped on account of ransoms which their loved ones are expected to pay to get them back. And in the case of the Nwosus, you cannot say they belong to the class of the manifest rich who would just issue a cheque and pull out millions from an account.

This family may live in a good house, they may drive state-of-the-art cars, but these are by no means out of the reach of anyone who has put in two decades of dedication into any career. And that brought the reality of the dangers that we are in closer home. As Yoruba people say, the death that kills your closest associate serves you notice of your own morality. If a journalist's wife could be kidnapped and a ransom of hundred million demanded, no one is immune to the kidnap madness. Fortunately, Toyin returned to her family four days after her abduction. Her release was followed by silence even though it was evident that some ransom was paid.

Five days after Mrs Nwosu's release, news went viral that Chief Olu Falae had been abducted on his farm on the day he turned seventy-seven—the kidnappers were neither respecters of persons nor their special days. Having served the country in various capacities, kidnappers could indeed assume that his family would be able to afford whatever ransom placed on him, but whither the respect with which this society held the elderly? Falae's kidnappers whom he identified as Fulani herdsmen further denigrated their captive's old age by slashing him with a cutlass and dragging him in the bush for several hours. That was in addition to the endless threats to his life in case they did not get the requested ransom.

Yet, this country moves on like there is nothing to worry about. Beyond the worn-out issuance of official statements condemning the dastardly act and promising to fish out the perpetrators, we do not see any concerted effort on the part of governments at all levels to check the rising incidence of kidnap and other violent crimes in the country. Every effort to tackle insecurity in the country appears to be concentrated on the Boko Haram insurgency in the north eastern part of the country but even this insurgency started on a minuscule level and only got escalated because no attention was paid to it.

Boko Haram started in one state in the North-East in 2002, leaders looked on without concern until it crept into other states within the region and soon became a national and, now, a cross-border problem that the whole world has to cope with. It is the same way kidnapping has festered like a sore. Starting with the activities of members of the Movement for the Emancipation of the Niger Delta (MEND) who mainly abducted expatriates in their attempt to sabotage oil installations, to the cruelty of Boko Haram members capped with the kidnap of close to three hundred school girls in April 2014, kidnapping has gradually become a franchise on a national scale.

In the past couple of years, states in the South-East became no-go areas on account of the rate at which prominent citizens were abducted sometimes from the comfort of their homes and without respect to age, sex or position in life. Prominent Nigerians that have been kidnapped over the past five years include ninety-two-year-old Dr Shettima Ali Monguno, one-time Minister of Mines and Power, who was kidnapped in 2013, on his way from observing jumat prayers at a mosque in Maiduguri. Before then, eighty-two-year-old Professor Kamene Okonjo, mother of the past Minister of Finance, Professor Okonjo-Iweala was kidnapped in Ogwashi-Uku, Delta state. Professor Hope Eghagha was adopted when he was Commissioner for Higher Education in Delta state. Anglican Bishop of Gwagwalada Diocese, Reverend Moses Tabuwaye was kidnapped on his way to Awka, Anambra state, for a church programme. Sheikh Adam Idoko, the Deputy Secretary-General of the Nigerian Supreme Council for Islamic Affairs (NSCIA) was kidnapped at Ogrute Enugu-Ezike while a popular columnist with *Vanguard* Donu Kogbara was abducted in Port Harcourt. *Daily Trust* suggested that Nigeria has recorded nothing less than 110 kidnap incidents in the past six months with total ransom demanded in the one billion Naira range.

Government at all levels in Nigeria can therefore not continue to look the other way while another form of insecurity takes over our land. My take is that the Buhari administration should give as much attention as it gives the fight against Boko Haram to the fight against kidnaps. This is the only way to nip the menace in the bud.

However, in the same measure that it considers the reinforcement of the country's security apparatus, government must also take the urgent jumpstart of this economy. The level of criminality which we currently see in Nigeria merely reflects the dangers that are inherent in youth unemployment, inhibited cultist practices and the derogation of our national values and ethos. These is however a tip of the evil that is ahead. Unless our leaders, political, community and faith-based, rise to the occasion and quickly come to an agreement on how to put an end to this disrespect for the humanity in all of us, these signs merely forebode greater catastrophe of our national failure as a people and society to appropriately respond to signs of the times.

The PUNCH
1 October 2015

Religion, Culture and the Plague of Domestic Violence

The reporting – and prosecution – of domestic violence has been on the rise recently. Take the case of Mr Lekan Shonde, who allegedly murdered his wife, Ronke. Even though there have been several cases of domestic violence since that time, that episode remains memorable for several reasons. First, it flew on the wings of social media into many people's homes. Second, the prosecution was also as public as the news itself.

While speaking from his hide-out, Mr Shonde painted his dead wife away as a shameless adulterer, who after the act, came to relive the salacious experience in her matrimonial home. He has presented himself as a caring husband, who took care of his wife, provided for her needs and only beat her once in a blue moon, the last time being three years before the slight push or was it hand brushing of her face on the day she died.

There were many inconsistencies in the narrative that do not always get our attention as we engage in emotional expositions and draw hasty conclusions; the same impetuosity is at the root of a substantial part of our troubles. The misunderstanding that led to the couple's last fight, did it result from the alleged sexual escapade of the late wife or her alleged presumptuous expenditure?

While domestic violence is a global problem, it has literally taken residence in Africa and is trailed by endless stories of pains and sorrow. It has become an intractable challenge, most likely to end or permanently damage the lives of victims and sometimes, their children. Accompanying this challenge are also questions on the role of religious institutions in the perpetuation of violent acts in the home. It is said that the persuasive authority of the clergy is employed to encourage women in abusive relationships to live it out, evidently because we think women should be found in the place of patience and long-suffering.

A friend recently told me of the story of a pastor who, matter-of-factly, told a parishioner to leave her abusive husband, even to the surprise of his counselled. Sensing the lady's surprise, he opened up on how he arrived at a point where he chose not to ever advise women suffering from domestic violence to remain with their abusers after the death of a church member. Despite repeated episodes of abuse at the hand of her husband, he counselled her to be patient. She was, until, her husband flung her to her death down the balcony.

But is the clergy really the devil in the circumstance? Although, I am mindful of arguments that religious ideas are part of the cultural heritage of a people, I would disentangle these related phenomena on a range of issues involving the management of relationships and situations by Africans

While it can be said that the religious beliefs of a people are an integral part of their culture, the embracement of Islam and Christianity has done everything but wean us off some of the cultural practices that our forebears were involved in before the advent of these two acquired religions. For example, I do not recall anywhere in the Bible where husbands got the authority to treat their wives like foot mats or punching bags. Adherents of the patriarchal essence of our culture find a convenient spot in the Book of Ephesians' passage that says: "...Wives, submit to your own husbands, as to the Lord. For the husband is head of the wife, as also Christ is head of the church..." But the same Scripture admonishes that: "husbands ought to love their own wives as their own bodies; he who loves his wife loves himself. For no one ever hated his own flesh, but nourishes and cherishes it, just as the Lord does the church." So, the husband is just a servant-leader here.

Concerning Islam, the recent eye-opening intervention of former Minister of Youth Development and Sports, Bolaji Abdullahi, on the gender equality bill is deserving of reference. He wrote *inter alia:*

On violence against women, the Qur'an states in 4:128, "if a wife fears high-handedness or alienation from her husband, neither of them will be blamed if they come to a peaceful settlement, for peace is best." On the holy book's prescription of mutual consent between couples on some issues, he informed: "...The notion of 'mutual consent and consultation' here implies equality between the couple, as there would be no need for consultation and consent if the God intended the relationship to be that of subordination..."

I suggest, therefore that most of the gender discrimination attributed to religion, actually come out of the muddling up the adopted religions and our cultural heritage.

It is in this society that the idea of dowry and bride price promote the proprietary complex of men over women and girls. It is in this society that the family structure is pervaded with the gender prejudice of the preference of boys over girls. This kind of society where girls have access to fewer opportunities engenders boys puffing the air of superiority into them, while we train girls to believe that they are good for nothing other than tending the stomach and making the bed of men, sometimes the age of their grandfathers. So, boys become men who would lord it over their women while women grow timid and unsure of themselves. This is the part of the world where we say women must continue to suffer just to avoid the stigma that we attach to separation and divorce.

While none of the major religions that we practise in Nigeria encourage the subjection of women, I do not excuse clerics who are unable to divorce themselves from the repugnancy of some of our cultural practices. Sometimes, I imagine how disappointed our forebears would be at the stagnancy of our ethos and our inability to recalibrate. No wonder, we have remained backward. Countries interested in development understand the importance of having all hands on deck irrespective of gender, and have progressively moved toward gender parity and the reduction of the vulnerability of women and girls.

Smart countries now understand the effectiveness of women in the improvement of their economic outlook and preparing for the challenges of the future. I think now is the time for Nigeria to jump on the train of change.

We should insist that our girl-children must be educated alongside their male counterparts. We need to bring up our children to see themselves as equals. We should train our boys to see girls as equal and make them understand that domestic violence is not only criminal but sub-human.

Parents and family members of women suffering from violence at home must desist from sending them back into homes where they have no peace either to avoid stigma or save their children. We must remember that only the living has a dignity to guard and children to rear.

In addition to educating girls, which should prepare them for future challenges, this society must brace up for institutional support for women who want to remain alive and leave their husbands. An essential strength of this country is its demographic advantage; gender disparity is one evil that would slow down Nigeria's development.

The PUNCH
12 May 2016

This Way, Nigeria is Not Going Anywhere

In *The Audacity of Hope,* President Barack Obama told a story that is impossible for me to forget. After his election into the United States Senate in 2004, he joined other senators at a breakfast meeting with President George Walker Bush. After eating to their fill and the meeting was coming to an end, Obama heard the President yell his name "Obama!" after which Bush beckoned on the Illinois Senator to come over for a brief chat.

The account in the book goes as follows:

"Come here and meet Laura. Laura, you remember Obama. We saw him on TV during election night. Beautiful family. And that wife of yours – that's one impressive lady."

"We both got better than we deserve, Mr President," I said, shaking the First Lady's hand and hoping that I'd wiped any crumbs off my face.

"Come over here for a second," he said, leading me off to one side of the room.

"You know," he said quietly, "I hope you don't mind me giving you a piece of advice."

"Not at all, Mr President." He nodded.

"You've got a bright future," he said. "Very bright. But I've been in this town a while and, let me tell you, it can be tough. When you get a lot of attention like you've been getting, people start gunnin' for ya. And it won't necessarily just be coming from my side, you understand. From yours, too. Everybody'll be waiting for you to slip. Know what I mean? So, watch yourself."

Obama thanked the president for the advice and the meeting ended. Four years, later, Obama was elected the first African American leader of the most powerful country in the world. What I find most interesting about this encounter is the fact that someone elected on the platform of the Republican Party could give such valuable advice to a politician from the opposing Democratic Party and prepare him for his future.

Every time I look at Nigerian politicians and their failure to come together and move the nation forward, I remember Obama's story in *The Audacity of Hope*. Is there even anything like national interest in the vocabulary of the average Nigerian politician? My experience over the years has brought me to the conclusion that nothing like that exists. For the Nigerian politician, what matters most is the interest of the self and his party.

Take the issue of the postponement of the 2015 elections over which Governors Rochas Okorocha and Olusegun Mimiko addressed the media. It seemed that the two main political parties which these governors represented went into the meeting with pre-mediated opinions which had nothing to do with the overall interest of Nigeria. Not just that, they also refused to be persuaded by any superior argument that may have been presented at that meeting no matter how much in the overall interest of the nation that might be.

How could leaders of a nation be like this? Perhaps, more disheartening and dangerous than the self-serving tendency of our politicians is the absence of a third intervening force in the country. Elder statesmen including former national leaders are so terribly partisan that none of them has the credibility to stand before Nigerians to propose options that may be acceptable to be people.

When you hear that old men like Pa Edwin Clark who was a minister in the First Republic and Professor Ango Abdullahi, a former vice chancellor of the Ahmadu Bello University (ABU), Zaria are about to address the press, you can bet they would have nothing to discuss other than sectional interests which would most likely set one part of the nation against another. So is the media, members of the civil society, religious and traditional leaders. We are just a nation that thrives on selfish and primordial sentiments with no thought for the nation. No experienced, soothing voice to calm the hot and unreasonable blood of partisans. We are all in the race to find which side to align with.

This is very unlike the United States, for instance, where an organisation like the Alfred E. Smith Memorial Foundation gives the two most prominent presidential candidates during every election year, the opportunity to attend a dinner in a relaxed atmosphere where they take jabs and laugh at each other's follies during political debates and campaigns. They come out relaxed and friendly in the interest of the nation.

Here political parties are perpetually at one another's throats; their supporters are always holding weapons of war; campaigns are battlegrounds while elections is warfare. Worse of all, citizens cannot read through the selfishness of politicians, most importantly because there are no stabilisers of the polity, everyone for himself in Nigeria, God for us all. And I am just wondering, how does a country move forward that way?

The Danfo Driver in All of Us

I can imagine the self-righteous anger rising in many readers at the sight of this headline. I am sure many people would ask: "What the hell does this writer think he is talking about? How dare he compare us to danfo drivers?" I get it. But that is all that it is—mere self-righteousness, that disposition that makes us forget that we are human and fallible. After all, isn't it said, that "to err is human?" So, if you are honest with yourself and patient enough to go through this piece, I am positive that it will make sense to you. At the end, you might discover something that you can do better to contribute positively to national development.

For so many reasons, Lagos is often described as microcosmic of Nigeria. One of the reasons is because you would possibly find someone from every ethnic group in Nigeria in the city of Lagos.

Danfo driving in the city is another peculiar phenomenon of the former capital city of Nigeria. The danfo is the ubiquitous yellow commuter minibuses that you find on Lagos roads. About two years ago, the Lagos State government said there were seventy thousand of such buses in the city, and threatened to remove them in their determination to impose sanity on the city. Everyone in Lagos has one bad tale or the other to tell about the danfo driver, who is in fact a representation of all that is wrong with the city. He signifies several things that most of us do not want to imagine about ourselves. Lately, I have been pondering over this issue and I wondered if the attitude of the danfo driver is different from the behavior of the average countryman. Apart from the intervention of time and chance that places different people at different levels of opportunity, the danfo driver, to my mind, is the archetype of the average Nigerian.

One of the things that you first notice about the danfo driver is that he cares only about himself. Owing to competition from his co-drivers, he has trained himself to believe that swiftness gives him an advantage over other people. The greater the number of bus rounds he makes, the more dividends for the day, especially when he makes daily returns to a bus owner. Therefore, anything that stands in his way bears the risk of being run down. If it happens to be another danfo driver, they would fight to the finish; if it is vehicular traffic, he is ready to run against the tide. He is prepared to do anything and as far as he is concerned, he is the only one on the road and that is exactly how he drives his bus along. When anyone, no matter who he is, contests ownership of the road with him, he is ready for war. He thinks he must always have the advantage and when that does not happen, he is determined that no one else gets it. So, he blocks the road, and everything comes to a halt for as long as it takes for a sane person to appear and assuage the ego of the danfo driver, or for a man in uniform, whip in hand, to come shout him down. Only then, does he get some sense of decency.

Depending on the scale of our responsibilities, a lot of us are like this. For those who reside in Lagos, traffic in the city tells you the story of Nigeria. The average driver on Lagos roads sees only himself. It does not matter if he is a chauffeur or a top executive who loves to drive himself. He puts himself first and if he cannot be the first, everyone can as well be held up. This attitude is evident in every area of our lives. Our businesses, our careers and even our government. The businessman explores the inefficiencies in the system to exploit every other citizen. People hoard fuel at the slightest opportunity or embark on industrial actions without considering their responsibilities to humanity. Nigerians just want to make profit no matter the cost.

When people like this get into government, they appropriate everything that belongs to everybody for themselves and their families. People steal and cut corners. They deny millions of people the opportunities that could change their lives forever. We are a community of self-centered people.

It is true that there is suffocating poverty in the land, but poverty is not the same as outright callousness. Is poverty the reason why people burst pipelines and leave millions of their compatriots suffering? Is that why they vandalise power installations without care about what happens next?

We are also extremely impatient people. Like the danfo driver, who wants to maximise his bus rounds, we are always in a hurry to arrive at our destinations or attain targets. That is ordinarily not a bad thing if we toe the right line and pay the right dues towards attaining our goals, but we do not have the time for that. In our impatience, we are ready to circumvent every rule of engagement that has been set. We would manipulate our way to promotions and pay to get others to lose their opportunities. These days, parents are initiate compromises that will spring up opportunities that their children do not deserve. These two tendencies—impatience and manipulation—then lead us into being unruly.

Take our model, the danfo driver for instance, because he is in a hurry, he will drive against traffic and climb the kerb just to get an advantage over other drivers. He will overload his bus against regulation, just so that he can make some quick gains. If you were to ask him how he became a driver and if he has a driver's licence, you would learn that he likely did not go to a driving school and paid a tout to buy him a licence, even when he could not distinguish between the clutch and the brake. He might have casually graduated to take the wheels after he had hung on the door for two years as a conductor.

Most of us are no different from the danfo driver. We drive our cars without authorisation, refuse to obtain the required documentations for our cars, we even drive against traffic or compete with the BRT buses on lanes designated for them. Many of our compatriots, especially those in high offices feel too big to present themselves at licensing offices. They create the problems that make things impossible at the passport offices, and then they circumvent the same procedures. We are prepared to bend the rules to make life better for ourselves, yet we expect others, who are not as privileged as we are, to live by those rules.

We are always quick to place the blame for disorderliness in the country on our leaders. Sometimes, that makes sense, but the progress of a country depends on good citizenship, which is the combination of the leaders and the led. That becomes easy to accept when we realise that everyone who becomes a leader rises from this same society and take those tendencies with him.

Sometime ago, a lawyer friend of mine spoke to me about his determination to stop when the traffic light turned red because the incoming president had decided to lead by example. He said he battled with obeying traffic lights before because the outgoing president's convoy disobeyed the lights. This is amusing because my friend lives in Lagos where a governor observes traffic lights, so how come people looked to Jonathan rather than Fashola?

This is a charge to all of us. We owe ourselves the duty of renewal. Let us give our country a fresh opportunity to grow by offering responsible citizenship.

The PUNCH
21 May 2015

NLC and the Welfare of Nigerian Workers

I am not a fan of the Nigerian Labour Congress. Over the years, I have held the opinion that the central labour union dabbles into territories outside its scope. Sometimes, the NLC behaves like it was some opposition party to the neglect of the welfare of its primary constituency- the Nigerian worker. For instance, when I read that the NLC threatened to shut down the country if the Federal Government attempted to sell our moribund refineries, I wondered what point the NLC wanted to score.

Here are refineries that have become such an unmitigated drain on the country's resources. I have heard about the dilapidation of these refineries since the middle 1990s when succeeding administrations had spoken about some Turn Around Maintenance (TAM) or the other. None of the countless TAM efforts yielded any of the refineries to its optimal capacity with the result that the country imports refined petroleum to satisfy local consumption. That is in spite of the fact that about $1 billion was injected into the repairs of the refineries between 1999 and 2007. It also was alleged that another $5 billion meant for further maintenance of these facilities was misappropriated in the same 2007. In 2012, Petroleum Minister, Diezani Alison-Madueke was quoted as having told the Senate Committee on

Petroleum (Downstream) that the Federal Government had plans to spend another N251 billion on the repair of the country's refineries. These figures do not include the hundreds of billions of Naira that the country lost to daily shady deals from the importation of petroleum products and subsidy. How then could any group of people insist that this manifestly corrupt and inefficient system should continue to bog down the national economy to the advantage of just a handful of Nigerians? This further made me see the NLC in the light of the man who refuses to seek cure for his leprosy but would do anything to get ringworm off his skin.

How does the NLC see to the welfare of Nigeria's estimated eight million workers and their families? To my mind, the average Nigerian worker bears the burden of the trauma that the economy has become to all of us. Sometimes, he suffers more deprivations than his relations who are unemployed. Since 2007, minimum wage in the country has remained N18,000 and only federal government workers and just a few states are privileged to get this minimum wage. I think about the responsibilities that the worker has to cope with and further query the NLC and its leadership each time I read press statements and interviews on policies that government should carry out and what not. How does the average worker in Nigeria provide food, shelter and clothing for his family? How does he send his children to school? How do we get employers of labour to treat their workers like human beings?

You consider the situation with healthcare delivery in Nigeria and wonder how, about nine years after the introduction of the National Health Insurance Scheme (NHIS), only six million Nigerians have enrolled under the scheme. I always imagine how the Nigerian worker and his family cope with their health challenges. How the labour union has not thought about the possibility of getting state governments to embrace community health insurance on behalf of workers beats my understanding.

I think about hundreds of thousands of Nigerians who work in less than human conditions. I think about the thousands who work in non-unionised environments. How banks subject their staffers to untold conditions and how thousands of bank folks have been thrown into the unemployment market in the past couple of years, without benefits and without anyone to raise his voice on their behalf.

I wonder why the NLC assumes that it speaks for all Nigerians when it has not done much for the less than ten million workers that are in the country. Primarily, the duties provided for the NLC in its enabling laws are: To represent the general interest of its members on any advisory body set up by the government of the federation; To give advice, encouragement of financial assistance to any of its members in need thereof; to collect and disseminate to its members information and advice on economic and social matters; Promote the education of members of trade unions in the field of labour relations and connected fields and; To render any other assistance provided for under the article of affiliation.

I always wonder where a body which cannot take care of the interest of less than 10 million people garner the clout to flex muscles on behalf of 160 million Nigerians, I am also upset with what I see as the grandstanding of these guys in the labour union.

But the Comrade Abdulwaheed Omar led NLC recently did something that made my heart glad. In a bid to ensure that its members have access to affordable houses, the NLC has entered into partnership with Kriston Lally EPC Nigeria Limited, a private property developer to build a $6 billion or N960 billion worth of affordable housing estates for Nigerian workers in all the thirty-six states including the FCT. The plan is to build affordable houses for all willing NLC members, whose figure is put at eight million persons. The labour movement is worried about the forty million housing deficit that exists in the country as revealed by a United Nations study.

Although I do not immediately have the cost of the houses, it is good to know that subscribers are required to put down just ten per cent of the cost and pay the balance over a period which could stretch from between five and fifteen years, depending on the choice of the individual. The first phase of this commendable project will, according to available information be delivered in Abuja in December 2014. Programmes like this, which affect the lives of workers positively should pre-occupy the NLC more than interventions completely alien to their brief.

The PUNCH
11 April 2014

Rebuilding Nigeria, All Hands on Deck

Nigerians, home and abroad, currently bask in a sense of accomplishment over the results of the last presidential elections. To many of us, this would be the first time that our desire to put an end to one administration will come to fruition without someone terminating the dream before it began. We wanted change, and change we got.

Nigerians sure have reasons to pat themselves on the back. Fifty-five years after independence, this Fourth Republic, now sixteen years old, is the longest attempt at democratic governance. In addition, the 2015 elections would be the first time that the opposition would unseat an incumbent. There are therefore varying fronts on which celebration is allowed.

But before we get carried away, we should remind ourselves that the successful completion of general elections is only one step in the very long journey to the attainment of democratic governance. We should buckle up for the very long walk ahead.

One of the mistakes that attend equating democracy with successful elections is that we easily surrender to politicians. But there could be no error more gross. The truth is that not even the best of politicians put the interest of the common man above their personal or party interest. The day they are sworn in is the day they begin to work towards winning the next election and anything they do during their tenure is targeted at winning again and luring you into permanently turning over your lives. The electorate must read through them and become willing partners in the national development project of which the entrenchment of democracy is a key part. It is on this all-important front that a lot of African citizens fail as a 2008 survey in The Afrobarometer, a publication coordinated by an alliance of organisations suggests.

The survey, in seeing whether democrats are emerging to enable democracy to thrive in Africa focused on three major questions: Do Africans hold democratic attitudes and values? Do they demonstrate political knowledge and engagement? Do they exhibit democratic behaviours via civic participation? It concluded that democratic citizenship is weak in Africa. The report also showed that while a majority of Africans are interested in politics and discuss politics with friends and family, less than half of the people on the continent have high levels of political knowledge. It discovered that majority of Africans do not know the names of their members of parliament. Therefore, a lot of these discussions are based on inadequate information and sometimes, the imagination of some of the discussants.

What about civic participation which enables citizens to learn about politics and to influence political and policy decisions? How many Nigerians attend community meetings where issues affecting the communities are discussed with the likely result of raising those issues with the authorities? How many of us have ever thought of the idea of joining a demonstration or mass protest?

It is also a fact that many of us would rather belong to religious and social groups than consider membership of voluntary and civil society organisations which could improve our understanding of how government is run and give us platforms for effective participation in the affairs of our country.

Many Nigerians see government more like a parent than those elected and paid by them. Most of us do not believe that we should hold elected officials accountable. When things go wrong in our communities, the first port of call for most us would be our religious or traditional leaders or some rich man in the community. We never think of mobilising to approach the man that we voted into the local government council or into our state house of assembly. And when constituents do not put their elected officials to task, they are at liberty to run riot.

And then tax compliance. Payment of taxes is a key mechanism by which people could develop a sense of rights and ownership of their government but a lot of those who have the resources to pay still wait until they need something from some government office before paying up. Ironically, these are some of the factors that have shaped those western societies that we all love to talk about. These attributes are lubricants for the democratic machinery, yet we fall short of them.

But there is a future for us in democracy which is why every Nigerian should work towards building a democratic citizenry. Democracy is an organic system in which every part must do its bit for any chance of proper growth. Thankfully, there is a lot of liberalism in many homes these days. Children are given the opportunity to express themselves. This will hopefully translate into a future inhabited by uninhibited citizens.

Outside of the home, Nigerian children should begin to have a feel of the demands of a democratic society.

Democracy is not an event, it is episodic, it is a process which takes years to build and we need to start making conscious efforts towards that.

We should introduce key elements of civic responsibility into our school curriculum. Practical steps should be taken to prepare pupils for the demands of democracy. It is possible to introduce a process of elections, rather than selection in the appointment of class representatives and school prefects. Pupils should prepare manifestoes and organise campaigns to sell their candidacy. They should develop the sportsman spirit, so they don't grow up into adults who understand the responsibility of winning and have the grace to lose. Even as we have the change that we desired, there is a role for everyone to play in making the change permanent.

Nigeria's Human Capital and Vision 2020

Until last week, I did not realise that Nigeria still had a dream by the name Vision 2020. Please, do not blame me, the slogan that I have government people repeat frequently in the past couple of years is the "Transformation Agenda of this administration", I have heard so much of that that I have assumed that the agenda for transformation has swallowed up the vision for the big year.

But that opinion changed when I heard Vice President Namadi Sambo speak once again about this almighty vision for which a lot of notable Nigerians have made inputs. Sambo, while at the closing ceremony of the nineteenth edition of the National Economic Summit, organised by the Nigerian Economic Summit Group (NESG) and the National Planning Commission in Abuja, encouraged the need to diversify the Nigerian economy especially through agriculture and how that would contribute to the attainment of Vision 2020. Vision 2020 was launched in 2009 as an economic plan aimed at positioning Nigeria to become one of the top twenty economies in the world by the year 2020. The vision planned to combine the National Economic Empowerment and Development Strategy (NEEDS) of the Olusegun Obasanjo administration and the Seven Point agenda of the Yar'Adua administration to: Stimulate Nigeria's economic growth and launch the country onto a path of sustained and rapid socio-economic development and place Nigeria in the bracket of top twenty largest economies of the world by the year 2020.

Parameters to measure the attainment of this goal, according to the policy document would include a sound, stable and globally competitive economy with a GDP of not less than $900 billion and a per capita income of not less than $4000 per annum. The health sector is expected to sustain life expectancy at seventy years and reduce the burden of infectious diseases to the barest minimum, an educational system that provides competent manpower and opportunities for citizens to attain their maximum potential as well as a peaceful, harmonious and a stable democracy amongst others.

I have however been wondering for the past few days whether our leaders have the capacity to deliver this vision to us anytime in the next twenty years, not to talk of 2020. To start with, I believe that their setting the 2020 target itself is either borne out of some attempt to hoodwink Nigerians into thinking that something tangible was going on in the polity or the failure of people in government to realise the huge demands of such a promise, especially given the enormous burden of underdevelopment that Nigeria has carried almost forever.

Fundamentally for example, this country of over one hundred and sixty million people has battled to increase power supply beyond the four thousand megawatts mark in the past fourteen years. That is not to talk about the shambles that our roads are, the unparalleled difficult terrain under which we do business as well as the fact that corruption is literally a Nigerian citizen.

As devastating as the systemic inefficiencies listed above and many others which we cannot readily give attention to are to the attainment of Vision 2020 and the chance that Nigeria would ever attain development, by far more worrisome is the country's attitude to the development of its human capital. While it is true that all round the country, there are ongoing efforts to reduce the country's infrastructural deficiency at different levels of government, and that infrastructure is a very integral part of the development process, it is my humble take that the level of education and state of health of the human beings in any society as well as what is being done to improve same, speaks a lot about the country's readiness for development.

As the late Chief Obafemi Awolowo said in a speech, titled: "Man is the sole dynamic in nature", which he delivered at the convocation of the then University of Ife in 1974: "The crucial point, which I want our rulers, planners, and official advisers to bear in mind, is that man is the sole dynamic in nature: and that accordingly, every individual Nigerian constitutes the supreme economic potential which this country possesses..." He then went ahead to demand free education for all Nigerian children as well as the offering of preventive and curative medical facilities in every part of the country so that every man would be sound and ready to contribute to the development of the country.

Researchers looking at the experience of some Asian countries like India, Pakistan, India, Republic of Korea and Malaysia, which incidentally has worked at a Vision 2020 since 1991 noted in a paper entitled "Role of Human Capital in Economic Development: Some Myths and Realities" that: "a nation needs to have a minimum captious mass of at least seventy per cent or more literate population. What this means is that if an overwhelmingly large number of people in a country are literate, even with simple basic education as being able to read newspapers, this may open up the minds of the masses, possibly make them more enlightened workers and perhaps institute some element of discipline in them. These are, of course, some of the essential prerequisites for a large organised production to run efficiently and for leading to rapid growth through mass literacy, better prepared healthy workers and conducive investment friendly government policies."

Malaysia also regularly assessed its educational needs, and the prioritising according to its needs, such that at different times, the country has found itself giving priority to Applied Sciences and Applied Arts programmes, at other times it was research while at others it was pure science. With this determination by the end of the 1990s, literacy rate in Malaysia was ninety per cent while life expectancy was seventy-two years. It took well over twenty years of persistent investment in education and health care delivery for Malaysia to attain this level of accomplishment.

While Nigeria is still talking about overtaking countries like Italy, Indonesia and possibly South Korea in 2020, university lecturers have been on strike for close to two months now. Eleven million children are out of school without any clear-cut strategy to stop that tide; well over one million young boys and girls cannot get into higher institutions yearly and ethnic and religious distrust permeates the land.

Things are not better on the health front. As we speak, only Kwara and Lagos states have any community health insurance policy which takes care of the common man. The National Health Insurance Scheme of the government is underperforming while about fifty-three thousand Nigerian women and girls suffer mortalities or morbidities from childbirth annually. According to Save the Children UK, seven out of every ten children die before their fifth birthday while almost half of Nigerians die before they get to the age of sixty.

One major difference that I noticed between Nigeria's Vision 2020 and Malaysia's Wawasan 2020 is that while the former is mainly focused on economic growth, the latter is principally about the development of its people, apparently with the understanding that only a developed populace could engender an economic prosperity. Wawasan 2020 aspires for a united Malaysian society, a fully moral and ethical society, a scientific and progressive society, a fully caring society, an economically just society in which there is a fair and equitable distribution of the wealth of the nation and a prosperous society with an economy that is fully competitive, robust and resilient. In attaining all of this, it gives priority to the enlightenment and development of its populace and that has yielded tremendous results. On the other hand, Nigeria's Vision 2020 seems to be more concerned about economic growth over and above the development of its human capital. This is, to my mind the reason why that vision would not be achieved and why, unless we begin to pay attention to the development of our people, we may never really attain national development.

Newsdiary Online
13 September 2013

Why Government Should Declare a State of Emergency in Education

I am one of those Nigerians whose support for the incessant strike actions by the Academic Staff Union of Universities (ASUU) is qualified. Of course, I am in total agreement that the welfare of universities teachers could be better and that standard in our universities has been declining for years but I hold two things against ASUU's industrial actions.

Having embarked on strike for over two decades, I frankly think that ASUU needs to find more creative ways of dealing with the continuous renegade attitude of successive governments to agreements. When you have situations when students spend one or more extra sessions in school on account of industrial actions, I opine that ASUU's strike actions are fast becoming part of the same problem that they are meant to solve.

Secondly and perhaps more importantly, I shudder at the suggestion that strike actions by ASUU are towards improving the fallen standard of education in Nigeria. Again, there is no doubt that the educational sector in Nigeria is in need of urgent intervention, but I find hints that the solution lies more urgently at the tertiary level, as suggested by some people, rather curious. It comes across to me an indication of our tendency to treat the symptoms of a difficulty rather than its cause.

Even if university teachers in Nigeria suddenly become the best paid in the world and our campuses become blessed with the best facilities possible, the standard of education in the country would remain parlous if the wrong quality of students get admitted. So, if things get so bad that we do not even have enough suitable candidates passing matriculations examination into higher institutions, what would be the pride of our universities and their managements if Nigeria ever gets to that position? What victories would ASUU have won when thousands of our children are unable to attain university education because they cannot make a success of their secondary education or when those who are admitted are half-baked school certificate leavers who have manipulated their ways into higher institutions?

Although we do not seem to realise it, Nigeria is not too far from this post as we speak. Consider the dwindling quality of the results from the school certificate and matriculations examinations. The rate of failure in the 2014 Unified Tertiary Matriculation Examinations (UTME) is equally alarming. Of a little over one million candidates that sat for the paper and pencil and dual-based tests, only 47 scored above 250 while over 715,000 of the number did not attain the 170 mark out of a possible 400! However, there are worse things than the mass failure that we see at this level.

Over ten million children of school age are believed to be out of schools in Nigeria, in spite of the Universal Basic Education Act of 2004 which makes education free and compulsory for the first nine years of a child's educational career. Nigeria is the one of the countries with the worst record of enrolment, retention and completion of basic education in the world. The truth of the situation is that if something is not done promptly, these ten million children and so many other more will not attend higher schools whether ASUU goes on strike or not.

This is why I think that the stakeholders in the education must come together to fight for the revival of the educational fortunes of the country rather than pick up individual battles. They must force the hands of government at all levels to pay more attention to the education of future generation of Nigerians.

Most importantly, there is a need to take another look at the welfare of teachers across board. As we speak, many states in Nigeria are yet to start the payment of the agreed Teachers Salary Scale (TSS) to their teachers. These governments still treat teachers like social workers whose rewards "are in heaven". To treat teachers like this is to mortgage the future of our country. This is why we find second and third-class individuals who have no business imparting knowledge across our educational institutions; that is why we see the mess they make through mass failure in examinations.

In the interest of the country therefore, we must take a serious look at the quality of teaching at all levels of education but with more emphasis on the primary and secondary levels. We must quickly design a system that rewards good teachers and dispenses with bad ones promptly.

A corollary to this is to the need to pay attention to teacher training. Why do we no longer have teacher colleges where people obtained Grade II certificates before proceeding to Colleges of Education for their National Certificates in Education (NCE)? Governments should strengthen these levels of training while the

Teachers Registration Council of Nigeria (TRCN) should take the business of regulating the profession more seriously.

Then, we must find a way to educate hundreds of thousands of youngsters who do not do not make good grades in their school certificates and matriculation examinations. Technical and vocational education could empower the Nigerian youth with important skills rather than turning to commercial motorcycle riding or violent crimes.

As Nigeria continues to seek the change it yearns, it is important that we give adequate attention to the education to every generation of Nigerians living at any particular time. It is the only investment with a sure interest.

The PUNCH
12 December 2014

The Futility and Danger of DSS Raid on Judges

According to the late Justice Chukwudifu Oputa, JSC, "No one should go to the Bench to amass wealth, for money corrupts and pollutes not only the channels of justice but also the very stream itself. It is a calamity to have a corrupt judge… When justice is bought and sold, there is no more hope for society…"

That was at a time when robust intellectualism dwelled among justices of our apex court. Their judgments had the force of law, became the law and made anyone associated with the practice of law proud. Yet, corruption existed in the judiciary otherwise Oputa would not have offered this profound opinion. But Nigerians have recently become more conscious of not just the activities of corrupt judges but the negative outcome they bear on national development. President Muhammadu Buhari has seized every opportunity to voice his frustration with the judiciary over his administration's avowed determination to wipe corruption out of the psyche of the Nigerian. A fortnight ago when he delivered a speech to commemorate Nigeria's independence, Buhari prayed: "… not for the first time, I am appealing to the judiciary to join the fight against corruption." Little did the nation know that the president already had already run out of patience and had incubated an unprecedented upset in the nation's judicial landscape. Seven days after this request for collaboration, Buhari authorised an operation in which operatives of the Department of State Services marched to the homes of seven judicial officers, two of whom are Supreme Court Justices. The secret police would eventually address a press conference where it accused the arrested men of corruption and claimed that staggering sums were recovered during the dead-of-night attack on the homes of these judges.

Since Saturday when the news of the encroachment and arrest broke, arguments mostly hinged on emotions rather than reason have raged amongst Nigerians over whether the mode and time of arrests conformed to the rule of law or not. Those who are sworn to swim or sink with Buhari hold that the rule of law could suffer as long as actions taken move the president's desire to fight corruption forward. Those opposed to the president insist that the DSS action was irregular indicating that the nation was only one breath away from full blown dictatorship. Fortunately, though, there is an accord that corruption in the judiciary is a cankerworm presently gnawing at the soul of the nation.

But that is about the only sense that you can make of the preponderance of interventions. Most of the arguments on this matter lack the intellectual rigor this matter deserves. The same way in which those who claim to fight corruption imagine that brutish actions would solve the challenge. How do we even expect the judiciary to be exempt of corruption in a country where everyone, including the politician, teacher, lawyer, journalist, doctor and even the clergy and traditional institutions are complicit in this culture of compromise?

How do we expect an immaculate judiciary in a country where the executive and legislative arms live large and consider themselves above questioning and accountability? Is it not the same Buhari who once alluded to not being able to afford his party's presidential nomination form that can suddenly afford to send his children to expensive schools abroad and tell Nigerians so with gleeful arrogance? Didn't the president promise to publicly declare his assets but began to amend his position when we got to the bridge? How does government hope to come to equity without clean hands? A more rigorous investigation, which is the only way to institute sustainable victory over corruption, would show that not just the Bench but the Bar and judicial administration, which includes registrars and the likes are involved in practices that subject justice to petty transactions. They would be more contemplative in finding solutions and realising that not even taking out all the judges in Nigeria would put an end to this dishonourable state of affairs.

One of those more temperate but ultimately impactful ways would have been to observe the constitutionally laid down procedures of allowing the National Judicial Council deal with erring judicial officers. The president and those who serve him, instead of serving the nation, should have known that there could be nothing more corrupt (not even the inducements allegedly received by the judges) than the circumvention of the legal provisions of attaining any purpose in a democracy. Such impurities are precursors to all forms of corruption.

Contrary to claims that the NJC refused to cooperate with the DSS, correspondence between the two bodies as published by *THISDAY* newspaper on Tuesday showed that the decision to adopt arbitrary self-help could have been due to nothing but the immodest self-worth of the DSS authorities who thought the NJC overreached by addressing the DSS Director General by his name while exchanging letters. Questions should have been asked about how people even become judges in Nigeria. Unlike in those days when judicial appointments were founded on the intellect, character and competence of people, politicians now appoint lawyers who are loyal to their causes to the bench; hence, the foundation itself is faulty. Had the president been more conscientious in this bid, he would realise that the working conditions of judges make them susceptible to venality. He would initiate a comprehensive reform in the mode of what his deputy, Prof Yemi Osinbajo, inspired as the Attorney-General in Lagos state. Do they even discuss these issues?

The president would have known that judicial officers are mostly overworked and underpaid in Nigeria and that a lot of them have become contractors, contrary to the ethics of their calling but in conformity with the realities of the Nigerian economy where every man is for himself. President Buhari would have seen that judicial officers make enormous sacrifices for the country, work under strenuous conditions, handle multiple cases, sit for hours, days on end, write manually and retire without being able to practise law again or even have so much of a voice to be heard. He would prepare for the nation to honour the honesty and selfless service of judges. Unless the president desires to selfishly tower above all Nigerians in honesty and integrity, he would realise that societal problems do not go away by fiat but by the creation of a framework of continuous collaboration, cooperation and engagement with every important component of the societal structure.

These are lessons that one thought he would have learnt from the premature expiration of his War Against Indiscipline the moment he was overthrown in 1985. Consensus building lubricates democracy and causes societal problems to evaporate like boiling water. Has the president ever considered meeting with heads of the other arms of government in a convivial atmosphere where they can rub minds and he could sell his vision to them and take their ideas? Or does he think he has all the answers? Now, this is no endorsement of the evil that corrupt judges perpetrate when they pervert the cause of justice. There, surely, could be no greater evil than the commercialisation of the last hope of the common man, but the process of arresting the evil must itself be wholesome and sustainable.

Finally, there are two things that Buhari must realise: no country facing economic challenges needs the kind of tension that the abuse of the rule of law currently generates in Nigeria. Giving security agencies the leeway to trample on the judiciary will encourage a new level of recklessness that this society may never be able to reverse.

More importantly, the government of a country cannot afford to desecrate its judiciary. In dealing with the unacceptable level of corruption in Nigeria, government must work with the structure that we have in place or propose a change to the legislature. Giving the impression that this structure is corrupt and useless is to sell the institution cheap and deny it the respect of Nigerians and foreigners as we have done the police. It will take generations to overcome such a disaster. The only way President Buhari can help Nigeria is to form a movement of believing stakeholders who will work with him to terminate this evil sustainably. That is how to leave an enduring legacy.

The PUNCH
13 October 2016

National Development and Local Government Administration

In the twilight of the Obasanjo administration in 2007, the former president awarded a contract for the construction and equipping of 774 comprehensive health centres. The project which was intended to improve healthcare delivery at the grassroots was meant to see one model primary health centre in every local government area in the country. Although the contract fell short of constitutional provisions and fiscal discipline of a federalist state, which made the Yar'Adua administration cancel it, the old man sure had reasons for his action.

I can also hazard a guess. Obasanjo, given his role in local government reforms in the past must have recalled that local governments were the closest to the majority of Nigerians and that access to primary healthcare facilities would increase access to quality healthcare especially by rural residents. He must also have identified the inability of council chairmen across the country to initiate such projects since the 1999 constitution makes councils mere appendages to state governments, who may not all be interested in pursuing such projects at that time. Anyway, the contract was cancelled and the health centres were never built. Leaving Nigeria's rural populace – seventy per cent of the country's population – worse off, as local government administration remains the only way through which people at the grassroots can see themselves as part of government, an essential ingredient for participatory democracy.

Apart from being in the best position to cater to the primary needs of the rural populace in the areas of health, education (including adult and vocational), agriculture among others, local government administration is also supposed to be a two-channel of communication between the local communities and the other two tiers of government. For many, local government administration justifies the definition of democracy as the government of the people, by the people for the people. All these are services, satisfaction and opportunities that the bulk of Nigerians have missed since the country returned to democracy in 1999.

The major culprit for the castrate state of local government administration is the 1999 Constitution and its legendary confusion. Although it guarantees the existence of system of local government administration in S7 (1), it donates the right for the determination of the structure, duties, composition and finance in the same sub-section to the state through its legislature. The constitution confuses us further when it states in S7 (6))b): "the House of Assembly of a state shall make provision for the statutory allocation of public revenue to local government councils within the state even though the provision immediately preceding that states as follows: "the National Assembly shall make provisions for statutory allocation of public revenue to local government councils in the Federation".

The lacunas in the 1999 Constitution have given state governors the opportunity to tinker with the existence, structure and finance of local government councils all over the country. By far the most paralysing of the steps taken by governors is the cornering of the financial allocations of the state through what is known as the State Joint Local Government Account. This situation has made it impossible for most local government councils to embark on capital projects that would impact on the lives of their people.

Expectedly, attending the possession of the finances of local councils by state governments is the total emasculation of the structure and composition of the councils. With the aid of their houses of assembly, governors' control of the state electoral bodies that conduct elections into councils. That is when elections are allowed to hold. So, year in year out, state governors select their cronies, people who would do their bidding and foist them on the local people without consideration for wishes of the people. These characters could also serve as caretaker committees who are only accountable to the governor and the House of Assembly when the governor so chooses.

This is why governors would not support the autonomy of local government councils. They have enjoyed their overlord status for so long that a termination would be unthinkable. Sound bites from Governors Rotimi Amaechi, Kayode Fayemi showed where the hearts of our governors are on this matter. At different fora in 2013, the two of them presented arguments ranging from the considerable, to the selfish and the insignificant to support their opposition to autonomous councils. None of these arguments contemplated the import of autonomy on the rural populace; none of these arguments addressed how granting autonomy to local councils can speed up the attainment of the Millennium Development Goals most especially MDGs 2, 4, 5 and

6. It is indeed ironic that state governors who complain about the federal government's attempt to emasculate them would want to control everything in their own states.

While one concedes the theoretical positions of authorities like KC Wheare that a federal state strictly has two federating units, Nigerian politicians and politics are of a different stock. The urge to win at all costs, the desire to appropriate any semblance of power within their reach is the reason we have not had any impactful governance in our councils in the past few years. In spite of whatever anyone says, the developmental challenges of Nigeria are more enormous than to expect that state governments would reach every nook and cranny of their states, this is why it is important for people in the local areas to be in a position to elect their own representatives. Not even the suspicion between the federal and state government should rob the masses the opportunity to feel the impact of government.

Any meaningful reform must address the mutual suspicion between the federal and state government such that councils are not used as agents of destabilisation in states. It must look into the composition of the electoral bodies responsible for elections into the councils. To ensure that the people's choice is relevant, state governments should have no role in the composition of this body. This would save us the distrust which has followed virtually every local government election that we have had in this political dispensation. You always find yourself asking how the Governor's party ends up winning elections all the councils in all states.

The review of the constitution must also make the indiscriminate removal of council officials from office by state governor impossible forthwith. For the sake of uniformity, the tenure, composition and functions of these councils should also be stated in the constitution such that councils can concentrate on the very important mission of taking development to the rural populace.

One should ordinarily assume that members of the National Assembly will overwhelmingly endorse the autonomy of local government councils, given the preponderance of opinion in favour of the provision and its expedience for the rounded national development, but a deep knowledge of Nigerian politics would instruct otherwise. To borrow the words of American industrialist, Henry Ford, "the only motive that can keep politics pure is the motive of doing good for one's country and its people." That is our appeal.

The PUNCH
1 June 2013

We Kill Militants but in Vain

Towards the end of 2018, American multinational, General Electric, published the result of a research on the future of work in Africa. The document, "Skills White Paper", made projections into the enormous potential within the continent and what it needs to do that could make the region the beautiful bride of the second half of this century.

Titled "Building Strong Workforces to Power Africa's Growth", the document, quoting the International Monetary Fund, suggests that by 2025, sub-Saharan Africa will be home to twenty-five per cent of the global population of people aged twenty-four and younger. It submits that successfully providing jobs for this population "will directly raise per-capita income, due to the resulting decrease in the non-working population."

And since working people typically save, there would be greater domestic savings providing money for investment, which would aid immediate and future growth. The paper also notices that the gainful employment of this population will lead to a fall in fertility rates and impact on the participation of the female gender in the labour force, lower the number of children per family and free more money to spend on the education and health care needs of families. The document is however generous in its honesty as it gives insights into the flipside of not managing this demographic dividend well. It says, "...without the requisite investments in skills development along with infrastructure and services, a growing proportion of youths could be left unemployed and with little hope for socio economic advancement. This could increase social tensions, undermining cohesion and stability."

As Nigerian military forces routed elements of the Boko Haram terrorist group, which had held the north-eastern part of the country hostage for about seven years, killing close to thirty thousand people of all ages, religions and tribes, a variety of similar insurgent and violent groups has emerged over the past couple of months.

We have the murderous Fulani herdsmen who at the last count would have snuffed life out of over three thousand Nigerians from several parts of country without as much as one arrest made. In addition to killings, they have been accused of kidnappings as well as raping women and girls. There is a perplexing audacity to the murderous activities of these herdsmen who take over rundown communities in what looks like an expansionist mission.

While agitators in the oil producing Niger Delta of the country cannot be readily accused of large-scale assassination, kidnapping and sexual molestation like the herdsmen, they have dragged that part of the country into unimaginable tension and insecurity. In addition to that, the incessant assaults of groups like the Niger Delta Avengers on national oil and gas installations have brought more strain on the country's already dire economic situation, even as they have worsened power supply.

Although there have been reports of a rapprochement between government and militants, there is yet no concrete deal that that would hopefully lead to the cessation of hostilities. That is worrisome as reports filtered in that government may be considering military action – similar action had been carried out in Ogun and Lagos states against militants who had terrorised coastal communities. Reports earlier in the week indicated that no fewer than a hundred suspected militants were killed in a three-day aerial bombardment initiated by the military to flush out pipeline vandals and militants operating at Ishawo, in Ikorodu, and Igando areas of Lagos state, and Arepo, Wawa, Elepete and Ibafo areas of Ogun state.

Aside from relentless vandalism and sabotage of oil installations, these militants are believed to perpetrate crimes including murder, kidnappings, rape, armed robbery and intimidation of residents in a wide range of areas within Lagos and Ogun states. The activities of these folks have turned many Nigerians into refugees in their own country such that the decision by government to flush them out of their hideouts would appear the most appropriate response in the circumstance. But the questions to ask are whether military action solves the problem perpetually and how many such internal deployments our military forces can accomplish at any particular time especially as pockets of violence erupt from various parts of Nigeria serially.

One of such incidents was reported by *The PUNCH* newspaper with the headline: "Teenagers invade Lagos streets, kill worshipper, loot shops on 11 July 2016." The story informed that fifty hoodlums, mostly teenagers, invaded five streets on the Lagos Island, killing one man, maiming others and embarking on a looting spree in broad daylight. They were armed with daggers and machetes with which they wreaked havoc on anyone in sight.

There is a group called "one million boys" that terrorised several towns within Lagos state at the beginning of the year. Although law enforcement agents have largely clipped the wings of the marauding gang who hurt, raped and stole with abandon, three members of the group were arrested later in the Ajangbadi area of the state. The point is that unless we deal with the situation that breeds these young deviants, military actions can never solve the problem in a sustainable way. For instance, reports indicated that some of those who got out of the military onslaughts alive have started regrouping in Ondo state. We are merely treating the symptoms with these military actions.

Former President Olusegun Obasanjo put it succinctly when he met with a delegation from the Economic Community of West African States (ECOWAS) by saying that West Africa sits on a keg of gunpowder with the level of youth unemployment in the sub-region. This is one of the points that I think Nigeria needs to urgently contemplate alongside military action like the one in discussion. According to a 2012 survey of the National Bureau of Statistics, youths in the fifteen to thirty-five age brackets were nearly seventy- million of the one hundred and sixty-six million Nigerians then. Fifty-four per cent of this number of youths were unemployed as of August 2014. Hundreds of thousands of more youths will join the number over time, and what does a country expect when the majority of its most productive population have no jobs and practically nothing to hope for?

There is also the issue of young school leavers who are unable to gain admission into higher institutions while the nation offers no alternative for them. Although Nigeria is said to have a total of four hundred and thirty higher institutions with 520,000 admission spaces, as of 2013, a total of 1,735,729 sought admission in that year alone. The implication is that about 1,200,000 youths were unable to gain admission that year, a situation that has not improved till date. Nigeria is neither able to get most aspiring young ones into higher education postings nor provide employment for hundreds of thousands of those who graduate from institutions yearly. We therefore have a crowd of agile, restless but idle and angry youths on our hands.

My suggestion is that the country works towards providing more opportunities for its young ones to get educated. If children do not get formal placements, a serious country must provide alternatives for them. Serious attention also needs to be paid to providing gainful employment for the youths especially as the country is diversifying its economy. What about exploiting the massive opportunities in agriculture, entertainment and sports? Nigeria must also deliberately re-orientate its youths, discouraging the get-rich-quick-by-all-means mentality that has possessed the soul of our nation.

The PUNCH
4 August 2016

PART THREE

2015: Are We Seriously Begging Jonathan to Run?

To be clear, I have nothing against President Goodluck Jonathan or the tendency that he would take another shot at office in 2015. For me, it is within his right as a Nigerian to so aspire, at least as long as no competent court of the land says otherwise.

Current political dynamics in the country indicate that Jonathan is the candidate to beat, if he chooses to run. Now, concerning this last point, it seems so obvious that even a blockhead would realise that Jonathan desires another term. I believe the president and his men have given us enough signals, what politicians call body language, to assure us of his plans for 2015. This is why I am unable to understand the endless parades and visitations calling on the president to run, endorsing him for a second term or collecting millions of signatures which compel a man who is in apparent romance with the office that he has held for about four years to run again.

The current wave of activities in support of Jonathan's vying for office in 2015 is at such a dizzying speed that one would have to pause every now and then to understand it. The confusion on the issue is on a number of fronts some of which I will presently attempt to discuss in no particular order.

Earlier, Special Adviser to the President on Political Matters, Prof. Rufai Ahmed Alkali was quoted as saying that about 8,000 groups are currently rooting for the President to contest in 2015. Rufai went ahead to say that:

"Indeed, initially we printed 5,000 forms that were distributed to the NGOs and other support groups, but the forms soon ran out and we had to print additional 2,000. As I am speaking to you now, we have at least another one thousand (1,000) groups demanding to be screened…we shall undertake content analysis of the reports with a view to properly positioning the various support groups for the challenges of the 2015 general election…We want to assure every support group irrespective of their sizes, from two-man group to 20-million-man group that they are all important to us and we shall carry them along."

So, I asked myself, is this man not supposed to be a public servant? Or am I missing something? It is the same question that comes to mind each time I see Secretary to the Government of the Federation, Senator Pius Anyim shouting himself hoarse at the rallies of the Transformation Ambassador of Nigeria (TAN) arguably the most prominent of the support groups for the 2015 Jonathan bid. So, at what point did these two gentlemen, who are experienced in public service, mix up the duties of the offices that they hold with that of service to the 2015 ambition of the president? Well, unless they are of course trying to flaunt it in our faces that the presidency initiated and funds these groups to create a sense of popular desire for him. Unfortunately, as repulsive a contemplation as this is, it appears to be the case, given the fact that Anyim has represented the president at each of these TAN rallies. Imagine the presence of the president at a rally meant to beg him to contest in 2015. Does that even sound decent?

If we ignore the demeaning involvement of Anyim and Rufai in this charade, you are forced to ask yourself what the motive of this endless agitations could be. One day, TAN would call out millions of deprived Nigerians to a rally despite the risks that the administration's health minister had told us are imminent in such large gatherings. On another day, leaders of the National Association of Nigeria Students (NANS) will counsel First Lady Patience Jonathan to broach the imperative of a Jonathan candidature during pillow talk. The next day, it would be the turn of some group known as the Goodluck Initiative For Transformation (GIFT) to threaten to sit under some tree in Abuja until Jonathan heeds their demand for him to contest in 2015 and make a declaration promptly. Like anyone cares what they choose to do with their time.

Of course, someone would argue that the travellers are merely exhibiting their freedom to associate and that would be true but we would also be right to pose a question at them: why do we need to beg one of 170 million Nigerians to continue to stay in office and on behalf of all of us? Especially when he has not given us any sign that he would not want to stay?

This brings me to the lack of originality in these initiatives and the attendant lack of credibility in its wake. Nigerians would remember that the last time we were subjected to such pathetic patronising displays was during the regime of late General Sani Abacha. Bringing back memories of Daniel Kanu and his Youths

Earnestly Ask for Abacha, these current day merchants have stepped up the game. While Kanu set a one-million-signature target for himself, TAN is determined to mobilise ten million signatures.

Currently, the organisation is inching towards its ambition. After that, we can anticipate the next spectacle that Nigerians would be subjected to. There would be a grand event in Abuja, possibly at the Aso Rock Villa where the president and his foot soldiers will be present. There, the leader of TAN would approach the president after numerous condescending speeches would have been made by stalwarts of the ruling party. He would embark on an emotional genuflection, beg the president to accede to the request of these ten million Nigerians who have vowed that their lives and that of their generations depend on another four years of his presidency. And then the President would react in the opulence of his office, thank the ten million Nigerians for appreciating his transformation agenda and then insult our collective intelligence further with a promise to look at this request on its merit and get back to Nigerians at the right time. The hypocrites would applaud, and everyone will go back home feeling accomplished.

But the ridicule of the situation is that the joke would be on those who think they are playing games with Nigerians. The pretense that the message from TAN and others does not have the stamp of the presidency is as laughable as the suggestion that Jonathan needs some serious convincing to be part of the 2015 elections.

And it is an idea that supporters of the president should not have allowed to prosper. I think it goes to the root of the sincerity of the administration. And more than that, it raises questions about whether Nigerians desire a president whose choice to run is dependent on some sycophantic manipulation at this time of her history.

The PUNCH
5 September 2014

How the APC Shot Itself in the Foot

The tragedy that hit the ruling All Progressive Congress (APC) on Tuesday was predictable, only that it happened much earlier than expected. I understand that partisans would consider classifying Tuesday's happenstance as tragic or outrageous, but if such persons, tarry and get a bit more reflective, they would recall that the People's Democratic Party (PDP) was deprived of just half of what the APC lost earlier this week when Honourable Aminu Tambuwal emerged as Speaker of the House of Representatives on 4 June 2011. But that marginal loss was enough to signal the beginning of the end of the party's long reign. How then are we able to predict what could happen when a ruling party does not have the confidence of leaders of the two chambers of the national assembly from the very outset? I think it is tragic, especially for a party with so much promise.

But the APC had it coming. Hinging his decision not to interfere in the selection of leaders of the National Assembly on the change mantra on which he was elected, President Muhammadu Buhari had stated in clear terms that he was ready to work with whoever emerges from the two chambers. Yet, events have shown that Buhari was alone in the contemplation that change should indeed transform from a mere election slogan into an action word starting with the party.

Some party stalwarts apparently calling the tunes for members of the National Working Committee (NWC) insisted that two people namely Senator Lawan and Honourable Femi Gbajabiamila must emerge as Senate President and Speaker of the House of Representatives respectively regardless of the feelings of other party members who are interested in the offices.

Mock elections that they called went on in spite of the boycott of Senator Bukola Saraki, Honourable Yakubu Dogara and their supporters with the desired candidates of the powers that be declared elected.

From here, a couple of discomforting things came up about the APC. The first is that a party which came to Nigerians with promises of change betrayed the people by going about the selection of candidates for national offices with such draconian fervour. While it is okay that a party may want to resolve the multiplicity of aspirations for offices among its members, it is counterproductive for party leaders to maintain that only people of their choice would make it to the office, in spite of the interests of other eminently qualified people.

In the aftermath of the emergence of Saraki and Dogara as Senate President and Speaker House of Representatives respectively, I have heard murmurings of over-ambition from shocking quarters including spokesperson of the APC, Alhaji Lai Mohammed. But I wonder whether there is really anything so called amongst politicians. It is legitimate for anyone to seek to attain any office that they desire. If the party on whose platform such a person has any contrary idea, it behooves on the party to either present a compromise, compelling enough for the aspirant to reconsider or go defeat him in a free and fair contest. If both parties are unable to reach a compromise, it is within the right of such a candidate to pursue his dream. This is more so when Saraki and Dogara only asked for open internal elections instead of the elections skewed in favour of candidates of some party leaders.

In any case, wouldn't the desire of members of the NWC and their sponsors to decide who occupies these positions also amount to over-ambition if we were to employ the same standards? Another point suggesting that Saraki and Dogara would have good company if the over-ambitious tag sticks is that in spite of the enormous capital that the duo and others brought to the APC when they left the PDP in 2014, the party, by insisting that none of them was good enough to take the numbers three and four positions in the land, bares its disrespect for justice, fairness and equity. This is despite the realisation that no politician makes such sacrifices for the love of God. All politicians make moves which would ultimately further their career and these veterans know these but chose to be self-centered.

The second unfortunate fall-out of the scramble for power by leaders of the APC is that they left the president bare. Nearly two weeks after the swearing-in of President Buhari, key intervening positions like that of the Secretary to the Government of the Federation as well as that of the Chief of Staff to the President have not been filled. The reason for this couldn't be far from the struggle for relevance among various groups of people that formed the APC.

The result is that Buhari is left without quality advice. He is left open to wildfire, without the advantage of deniability for any step or misstep that he might make. This, to mind, would account for the reason why the president sent the order of proclamation to the National Assembly way ahead of the inauguration of the assembly. Were the party leaders more alert to the need to protect the president, such proclamation would have been withheld until possibly after the president's scheduled belated meeting with APC legislators. The president's letter to the clerk legitimised the seating of the senators that elected Saraki.

Tuesday's event should send a signal to the leaders of the APC that there is no one person with the exclusive blessing of strategic thinking. In actual fact, the master stroke of seeking the adoption of the senators elected on the platform of the PDP shows Saraki and Dogara as strategic political thinkers that the APC should not joke with. In addition to that, it suggests that those who opposed the candidacy of these two winners are actually not as adept as they appear to be. It is unthinkable that they imagined that their candidates would win the elections without the support of PDP members such that Saraki had them all behind him, no matter what he had to concede. After all, negotiation is one of the most important skills that a leader should possess, an asset that a political party should pursue.

Typical of the way politics is played in Nigeria however, the APC fired a salvo at Saraki and Dogara in statement issued by Mohammed which rejected the emergence of both gentlemen even as it threatened party sanctions on them. Let us hope that the threat will not go beyond the paper on which it was printed, and APC leaders would bury the hatchet and not allow their egos to overrun them. Evidently, the party will now want to preach the importance of party supremacy and discipline, but the truth is that enforcing such principles also demands a measure of impartiality from those who have the responsibility of leading the party. Without cleans hands, the leadership of the APC cannot demand equity.

The party hierarchy therefore needs to rein in all the burgeoning egos that have been bruised by the *coup de main* spearheaded by Saraki. Going ahead with the threat to reject the election of these men and sanctioning them will drag the APC into needless crisis which would be unhealthy for it and the nation. What I think the APC should concentrate is how to support President Buhari and the legislature in providing meaningful leadership to Nigerians.

The power tussle which will result from those threats will deepen the gulf of distrust in the party, push these gentlemen further away and set the tone for the failure of an administration on which Nigerians have placed all their hopes. It would also be the seal on the coffin of the APC and the ultimate tragedy, the kind which would make child's play of the confusion that visited the PDP after the March 28 elections. Let the APC save itself from this looming disaster.

The PUNCH
11 June 2015

In Memory of the Nigeria Governor's Forum

Unfortunately, I cannot qualify this headline with the word "loving" as I am not confident that many Nigerians would to testify to anything "loving" about the memories of the NGF. If we cast our minds back, we will remember that the NGF once played a role in the settlement of the crisis between the Nigerian Union of Teachers and the Federal Government in 2008. We will also remember that the forum played a significant role in the resolution of the unfortunate drama which engulfed Nigeria in the weeks before the passing on of the late President Umaru Yar'Adua in 2010. We also remember the battle of the NGF to protect federalism on the issue of the Sovereign Wealth Fund. But all that is ancient history, time has eroded these achievements; we cannot recollect any recent significance of the NGF to Nigerians rather than their connivance with the President to foist a fuel price increase on us in January 2011. Well, that is my own recollection; I don't know how many people agree.

I am also not sure that everyone would agree that the end has come for the NGF but that is how I see it. I do not know how anyone wants to claim victory in the scenario that unfolded this last weekend. Neither Governor Rotimi Amaechi nor Governor Jonah Jang has the full complement of the 36 governors in Nigeria, which was the basis for the NGF, so my point is that the

NGF as we knew it before the elections of Friday, 24 May 2013 does not exist again. And it may never exist again unless reason prevails.

But things should have gone this way. The NGF has every opportunity to have made itself not just politically relevant in such a way that it becomes a fright to presidents and political parties. It could also have courted the love of Nigerians. One of the major reasons why this group should be in existence is what they call peer review. My layman understanding of this is that Governors would compare notes, and replicate what works in certain states in other states after establishing best practices. If this had been the case, more states in Nigeria would have more happy people. A quick look at some possibilities.

Kwara state is said to be the innovator of commercial agriculture in the current political dispensation. Yet, how many states have looked at the model and started such ventures in relation to the resources in their states? Rivers state is said to have achieved a revolution in its educational sector, how many states have taken a cue from that? Ondo state is said to be leader in a revolution in the health sector, especially Maternal, Newborn and Child Health, how many states have studied the initiative taken it back home? Lagos and Akwa Ibom states are said to have done well in the development of infrastructure, has any state studied their models with a view to seeing how they can work? So, what is this peer review talk about?

There is however one way that peer review has worked across the states: in their collective anti-people decision to castrate local government administration. People can no longer choose their representatives at the local levels. The governors just impose. States like Osun, Delta, Oyo, Abia and Ekiti, and more, have even refused to conduct elections into the councils, that is what they do when they fear that they might lose elections. Those who conduct elections do so with the determination to win at all cost, all of it followed by serious acrimony as we have recently seen in Kogi, Edo and Lagos states. This is one of the reasons why primary education and primary healthcare have suffered greatly in Nigeria.

Maybe the NGF could have had another chance if its members were not just egoistic and undemocratic. How come some of the most important men in Nigeria, 36 of them find it difficult to reach an amicable agreement on how to ensure the survival of an organisation that they all love? What is the pride of Jang or Amaechi in leading a divided forum? Oh, the joy of working for the presidency and defeating the presidency respectively, I guess. How does that help the common man please?

A sitting chairman's refusal to dissolve the house before conducting an election is inappropriate in my opinion. And it is wrong to compare this to governors not stepping down before participating in general elections because governors do not preside over such elections, it is in the hands of an independent body known as the Independent National Electoral Commission and established by Nigerian Constitution. The NGF election is not the same, it is conducted by the secretariat which the incumbent has supervised for at least two years, come on! On the flip side, how do people submit themselves to a process and then cry foul when the process does not pay them? What the two parties have shown us very clearly is their lack of respect for democratic ideals.

If thirty-six people, who are leaders of their respective states and upon whom the survival of our democracy revolves, can conduct an election and come out with two different results, if these men can say one thing in the morning and deny it in the evening, then we should be afraid for the future of democracy in Nigeria. I agree that this may be in the character of Nigerian politics, but it is evident of leadership without responsibility. In any case where is the communiqué from the NGF after the elections?

It is equally shocking that the presidency or its apologists would get caught up in issues of a body which is not known to the Nigerian constitution. To my mind, such events diminish the office of the President to the detriment of our democratic growth.

The media has also not helped matters and I say that with a broken heart. I do not see how headlines about anyone flooring anyone as answers to the demand of objectivity placed on the media. Such headlines and so many others take the media into the arena and erode credibility. My knowledge of the operation of the media tells me that speculations are allowed but I am sorry, we very often take speculation into the realm of reality, colouring the minds of not just the parties but the electorate.

Ironically, the presidency and the Peoples' Democratic Party which we all want to spite might be the beneficiaries of this confusion, even though our emotions might deny us the sight of that fact at the moment. If the media is correct in the suggestion that these two bodies are interested in controlling the NGF, I opine that splitting the group would be as beneficial as having their stooge on the chairman's seat. All they would want is that Amaechi has no control over the governors and that has happened now. And for 2015, that is still in the womb of time.

When events like this happen, I remember the fear expressed by late statesman and politician, Chief Obafemi Awolowo that a certain generation may not witness democracy in their lifetime and fear overtakes me. That generation has definitely not seen democracy but would the generations after them? I say this with every sense of respect, but I do not think that anyone of us is helping the democratic cause. This is what putting the gun on the NGF's head by its own very members has shown me.

Omojuwa.com
24 May 2013

Nigeria's Democracy Without Democrats

Let me be clear from the outset, I love democracy and I believe that it remains the best form of government. What I am not certain of is how much of the democratic attribute exists in the average Nigerian. Let me explain.

Most of us grew up under very undemocratic conditions. Our fathers were the all in all at home and the only time that our mothers had a voice was when daddy was away. It goes to say that daddy's absence was the only time that the child could hope to whisper one or two things to mum. So most of us grew up in homes where we could not express ourselves, where we could not choose the people that we associated with. Even after we grow up and bring forth our own children, we mostly continue in the tradition, passing restrictions unto our children as a way of life. As this happens, we already would have missed out on the opportunity to cultivate some fundamental attributes of democracy – freedom of expression, freedom of association and tolerance as the case may be. It is just difficult for us to concede the rights of people to hold opinion, a man writes an article, or a book and we pour invectives on him and his generations.

So, the best of our politicians goes into public life with that baggage, no matter what education they acquire or progressive credentials they profess, they just cannot divorce themselves from these hang-ups. They must win elections at all cost; every candidate must bow down to their "godfathership" and the electorate cannot have any say in the way they govern. Worse still, they see nothing wrong with any of these. The raw use of power is just what they understand.

But we also are a largely passive citizenry, apparently a fall-out of our culture and the prolonged years of military rule. For democracy to grow, however, leadership and followership alike must understand, imbibe and demonstrate some democratic attributes. It is important for every citizen to come to grasp with these democratic demands because every leader emerges from the citizenry.

This is where my worry lies. What democratic credentials do our politicians acquire as ordinary citizens before they take on the responsibility of governance? How then do these leaders imbibe - or demand - any traits of citizenship in their followers. It is like asking them to give that which they lack.

Although many Nigerians say that they prefer democracy over military rule, it is also true that so many of us see government more like a parent than those elected and paid by us. Most of us do not believe that we should hold elected officials accountable, so our governments are unaccountable.

The Afrobarometer report showed that while a majority of Africans are both interested in politics and discuss politics with friends and family on a regular basis, (which is a good sign), less than half of the people on the continent (nineteen countries were sampled) have high levels of political knowledge. It discovered that majority of Africans do not know the names of their members of parliament. As a result, a lot of these discussions are based on inadequate information and sometimes, the imagination of some of the discussants.

What about civic participation, a factor in the sustenance of the democratic process which enables citizens to learn about politics and to influence political and policy decisions. How many Nigerians attend community meetings where issues affecting the community are discussed with the likely result of raising those issues with the authorities? How many of us have ever thought of the idea of joining a demonstration or mass protest? Gone are the days when the reactions of student and professional bodies to anti-people policies were spontaneous, you wonder today if you actually have a National Association of Nigerian Students among others. All we get are occasional rented crowds.

It is also a fact that many of us would rather belong to religious and social groups than consider the membership of voluntary and civil society organisations which could improve our understanding of how government is run and give us platforms for effective participation in the affairs of our country.

I have also noticed that when things go wrong in our communities, the first port of call for most us would be our religious or traditional leader or some rich man in the community. We never think of mobilising to approach the man that we voted into the local government council or into our state house of assembly. We do not realise that when constituents do not put their elected officials to task, they are at liberty to run riot.

What about the issue of tax compliance? As painful as the payment of taxes may be, it has been described as key mechanism by which people could develop a sense of rights and ownership of their government. It is the same way that the colonial masters pursued our great-grand fathers to pay taxes that government still pursues us today. And I do not mean people who do not have the wherewithal to pay taxes here, I am talking about those who have the resources to pay income tax, property taxes and local government licences but will wait until they need something from some government office and must fulfil the demand to present a tax clearance certificate before paying up. So why wait until you are forced?

Ironically, these are some of the factors that have shaped those western societies that we all love to talk about. These attributes are lubricants for the democratic machinery.

But I think there is a future for us in democracy. Since we love democracy, there is an urgent need for every Nigerian to work towards building a democratic citizenry. Democracy is an organic system in which every part must do its bit for the chance of a proper growth. Thankfully, there is a lot of liberalism in many homes these days. Children are given the opportunity to express themselves. This will hopefully translate into a future inhabited by uninhibited citizens.

Outside of the home however, Nigerian children should begin to have a feel of the demands of a democratic society. Democracy is not an event, it is episodic, it is a process which takes years to build and we need to start making conscious efforts towards that.

I am of the opinion that we should introduce key elements of civic responsibility into our school curriculum while practical steps should also be taken to prepare pupils for the challenges of democracy. It is possible for instance, to introduce a process of elections, rather than selection in the appointment of class representatives and school prefects. They should be encouraged to prepare manifestoes and organise campaigns to convince their school mates on why they should be elected. They should develop the sportsman spirit, so they don't grow up into adults who must win every time.

Yet we cannot give up on the adults. Government and civil society organisations should consider building democratic citizenship a necessary contribution to the entrenchment of democracy in the country by opening opportunities for Nigerians to get active in governance. The future will justify all such investments into the making of a free Nigeria.

Igbos, their Politics and the Rest of Us

Since the conclusion of the 28 March presidential election and emergence of General Muhammadu Buhari of the All Progressive Congress (APC) as winner, I have come across assorted commentaries on how the Igbo people of South-East Nigeria are the losers. About how they have lost the opportunity of a lifetime by voting for Buhari's opponent and not giving the APC the chance of winning just one single senate or house of representatives' seat in the zone. Some of these criticisms, the most scathing in fact, have come from native Igbos themselves and so you are lured into taking a keener look at the issues.

Simply put, the point is that if Igbos had voted for the APC, thereby joining the three zones in the North and the South-West zone in not just giving the day to Buhari but also returning people like Dr Chris Ngige into the senate, the zone would have been in good stead to clinch the Senate Presidency – the number three seat in the country. But that is not going to happen. Neither would the zone have any chance at presenting the first among equal three hundred and sixty members of the House of Representatives.

So, a lot of Igbo men and women and a lot of their friends sympathise with this remarkable group of people for the wilderness that they would be for the next four years. On the flip side, those who have never seen good in the Igbo gloat over yet another evidence of the tendency of the Igbo people to orchestrate their own undoing. If you live in a country where credentials for leadership is mostly hung on descent like Nigeria, you would most definitely understand why some would mourn while others rejoice at the inability of a major ethnic group to take its position in the comity of groups. As it is, the loss of the Igbos is the gain of some other ethnic group that "delivered".

Most analyses that I have encountered tried to identify reasons why the Igbos would almost always find themselves in this place of dryness. One of the very common arguments that I have heard in the past two weeks is that the Igbos are legendary at not being able to speak with one voice. In other words, they are so opinionated that they are unable to aggregate opinions in the interest of their kin.

The second argument is that Igbos do not trust the two other major ethnic groups to wit, the Yoruba and the Hausa essentially as a fallout of their collaboration against the former during the civil war, which ended forty-five years ago. They are also accused of always putting their eggs in one basket. But I find these arguments either impeachable or not peculiar to Igbos. The first, in my opinion is, not sustainable beyond its mention, at least as far as it concerns the 28 March elections.

Igbo speaking people of Nigeria occupy the five states of the South-East zone and a part of Delta state which falls into the South-South zone. At the end of the elections, all these states without exception voted for President Goodluck Jonathan, candidate of the People's Democratic Party (PDP). Now, I do not know how a people could possibly speak in unity more than this. Unless we are saying that speaking in unity is equivalent to voting for the APC. But let us for a moment assume that the Igbos did not speak with one voice in the recently concluded elections, I want to suggest that they are not alone in this failure. I suggest that even the Yoruba of the South-West, in spite their eventual gain, did not speak with one voice on the presidential election. As far as I recollect, the only group that is known to speak for the Yoruba is the Afenifere and it indeed rooted Jonathan.

The prime position that the South-West finds itself today is through the effort of one man and his foot soldier governors. And I would be shocked if anyone suggested that these men were particular about the interest of Yoruba when they embarked on the venture that resulted in the emergence of this government. After all, it was this same set of people that denied the Yoruba the opportunity of sitting at the top of the House of Representatives in 2011. I am sure someone would describe that as strategising. And that may be right, but I will return to the subject later. Not even the North, which made up its mind to fight for the return of power which is the same as the presidency to Nigerians since 2011, could be said to have spoken with as much eloquent oneness as the South-East as Jonathan and his PDP still made some good show in the North-Central and the North-East. I also do not think that having all eggs in one basket was anything peculiar to the South-East during these last elections. The North-West and the North voted exclusively for Buhari while the South-South voted exclusively for Jonathan. It is only in the South-West and the North-Central that both candidates made gains.

On the inability of the Igbo to trust the Yoruba and Hausa/Fulani tribes, I suggest that the Igbo is not alone in the trade. People of the three major ethnic groups in Nigeria must be honest enough to agree that there is mutual distrust among them, and it is disingenuous to continually posit that it is only the Igbos that have refused to move away from the event of 1967 to 1970. More intriguing is that the Yoruba and Igbos seem to find it easier to move up north for alliances, rather than work with each other; a situation that has left the southern part of the country disadvantaged for long. But the north only trusts either of these group when it is convenient. It uses its number to manipulate them when it needs to and wields distrust when it suits it. It is in such mutual lack of confidence that Azuka Onwuka, situated events in an article published in *The PUNCH* on 4 November 2014 about some northern youths protesting an unsavoury cartoon published in faraway, Denmark by killing Igbo in the North and setting their property ablaze. I bet other people of southern extraction would have suffered from this fate, and most of the time this happens, there are retaliatory attacks from the South.

In effect, there is a reciprocity in the distrust that plagues Nigeria's major ethnic groups to the disadvantage of the country, because unless Nigeria brings out the best in its people, regardless of where they come from, the giant of Africa will remain stunted. Those who accuse the Igbo of not voting right in the last election advocate for a collaboration of the three major ethnic groups in Nigeria, which would have amounted to a conspiracy of the majority and an inherent entrenchment of the injustice that trails the history of this country. They accuse the Igbo of selfishness and lacking the capacity to think strategically like their Yoruba counterparts, insisting that therefore they may not take "power" anytime soon. But some questions agitate my mind when I hear these arguments. Does an ethnic group need to have people in government before it feels a sense of belonging? How far can Nigeria go with this level of strife despite its immeasurable resources. How does strategising on how to get members of your ethnic group into national office even help that group?

For instance, it is on record that the individuals from the North have governed for thirty-seven out of its fifty-five years yet the region has nothing to show for it except for grinding poverty and abject lack of opportunities. Courtesy of Northern Nigeria, this country has the highest number of out of school children in the world. This means that the North is not just lagging, it is not preparing for the future. Poverty is highest in the North-West and North-East of the country with rates put at 77.7% and 76.3% respectively. The condition of the woman in Northern Nigeria is among the worst in the world. It starts with lack of education, followed by early marriage cum pregnancy and the lack of adequate medical attention, which could lead to anything from lifelong deformation to maternal and infant death. What did the eight years of President Olusegun Obasanjo do for the South-West? Has President Jonathan's five years improved the lot of people of the South-South remarkably?

This is why I am hoping that the incoming General Muhammadu Buhari administration would do a good job of national integration. That it would address the structural imbalance in the country and give every Nigerian a sense of belonging irrespective of where they come from. I do not only see this as an important task, I see it as an urgent one, central to the success of the administration. These primordial sentiments and the prominence that they have gained in national life are at the root of some of the most disturbing problems, including corruption and mediocrity that beset our nation. Without bringing the tribes together, this blessed country of ours would go nowhere despite the potential that it holds for African and global development. Without bringing the tribes together, making everyone feel like an essential part of the country, this giant would remain a dwarf.

The PUNCH
9 April 2015

PDP and APC Should Stop Lying to Nigerians

When former French leader and statesman, Charles de Gaulle said that "since a politician never believes what he says, he is surprised when others believe him," he must have had the Nigerian politician in mind. Currently, our political leaders increasingly gravitate towards dispensing half-truths and outright lies to Nigerians rather than address the issues which directly affect the development of the country.

In the past couple of weeks, politicians across the divide have taken to incredible information manipulation not only to increase their own chances but to diminish their opponent's chances. The impression we get is that electioneering is war and since all is fair in war, politicians can embrace any weapon of warfare, without consideration for the negative effect of their methods. But elections should not be war, it should be the celebration of democracy.

Communications experts would say that our politicians have employed propaganda, but I insist that this tends towards an extreme fiddling with the intelligence of hapless Nigerians who desire urgent improvement in their standard of living.

True, propaganda which has its origin in the propagation of the Christian faith by the Catholic Church, is fair and effective in war. Volumes have been written on how effective propaganda was in the execution of the war which Hitler started on the world, for instance. Even Hitler gives us more insight into what propaganda is through his words: "If you are going to tell a lie, don't tell a little one because it will be recognised as a lie. Tell the biggest and most unthinkable lie." Nigerian history has also seen the effective use of propaganda during the civil war. We also saw the use of propaganda in the years of military rule and now, politicians are on a propaganda spree.

Richard Alan Nelson, an American communications educator describes propaganda as "a systematic form of purposeful persuasion that attempts to influence the emotions, attitudes, opinions, and actions of specified target audiences for ideological, political or commercial purposes through the controlled transmission of one-sided messages (which may or may not be factual) via mass and direct media channels."

Propaganda is generally an appeal to the emotion, not the intellect. It tends towards self-praise and is very prone to dismissing opposition with the ultimate aim of securing an uncritical following. Propaganda inclines towards being overbearing, dogmatic, assertive and disinterested in debate.

The People Democratic Party (PDP) and the All Progressives Congress (APC) appear to be racing at outdoing each other in the propaganda war. Let me give you two examples of stories that I found amusing and irritating at the same time in the past one week. Last Saturday, there was a news item alleging that the federal government planned to freeze the accounts of major financiers of the APC. The report credited to Mallam Shehu Garba, spokesperson of the All Progressives Congress Presidential Campaign Council (APCPCO) described the alleged plan as "bestial and undemocratic," calling on Nigerians to resist the move even though he showed no iota of evidence.

The next day, many Nigerians including very influential legal practitioners joined the fray, denouncing any attempt by the federal government to clamp down on the finances and aircraft of incumbent Governor Rotimi Amaechi of Rivers state and former Governor Bola Tinubu of Lagos state. In releasing this information, Garba totally forgot that identifying Amaechi, a sitting governor, as a major funder of the party's presidential campaign would most likely run against the laws of the land. But he said it and Nigerians, without raising questions, fell for it.

Not going to be outdone by the opposition, Garba's opposite in the PDP, Mr Femi Fani-Kayode alleged that the vice-presidential candidate of the APC, Professor Yemi Osinbajo had taken an oath to resign and make way for Asiwaju Bola Tinubu six months after assuming office. This was on the same day that chairman of the PDP alleged that the fuel scarcity being witnessed in the country was sponsored by some opposition leaders who he failed to name. I wonder how they come about these random talks.

Yet, there have been far more ludicrous, sometimes devious unsubstantiated claims from both sides. Just a few examples would suffice. After the emergence of General Muhammadu Buhari as APC presidential candidate, a medical report, purportedly emanating from the Ahmadu Bello University Teaching Hospital (ABUTH) indicating that Buhari was terminally ill from prostate cancer appeared on the internet. The management of the hospital later denied issuing the report. This was followed by an almost mindless campaign on the imminent mortality of Buhari spearheaded by Ekiti state Governor Ayodele Fayose.

The PDP also alleged, again without proof, that the APC merely used Buhari's appearance at Chatham House, London as cover for his ill-health. Fani-Kayode who raised this allegation further suggested that the party parted with about N5 billion to set up the speaking engagement. He insisted that Buhari was in the UK for medical purposes and that his presentation was hurriedly arranged and paid for. Some members of the PDP have also relentlessly tried to discredit Chairman of the Independent Electoral Commission (INEC), Professor Attahiru Jega, fuelling speculations of his impending sack, something that the opposition has also latched on to without any proof.

The APC had done its bit of misleading the public and whipping up sentiments against the PDP. There is the story of a picture of General Buhari which was said to have been presented to deceive for instance. No attempt has been made by all the vocal image makers in the party to deny insinuations that the media was manipulated into publishing this misleading picture in an attempt to show that Buhari's mission to London is not medical. But I cannot stop asking myself, what if he did attend hospital in London?

There is also the unsubstantiated claim that the Federal Government gave a six billion Naira bribe to pastors across the country made by Governor Amaechi. And another that the federal government was behind the Boko Haram attack on Gombe state on February 14, 2015. Leaflets urging people to stay away from the polling booths on election days were circulated during this attack.

The APC also alleged that the federal government plans to frame Buhari as a sponsor of the Boko Haram insurgency. This followed government's encouragement of the army to capture leader of the Boko Haram group, Abubakar Shekau alive. This weighty allegation is apparently the product of somebody's fertile mind as nothing has been heard of it again.

The allegation that men of the Nigerian military surrounded the Ikoyi, Lagos home of Tinubu was a ruse after all as no one has provided any proof, not even a photograph. Same goes for the insinuation that Jonathan planned to bribe members of the national assembly toward extending his stay in office by six months.

So, from name calling and mudslinging, the leading political parties have moved on to cooking up stories which fall flat when subjected to scrutiny. I am thinking that it is the time for politicians to speak to the needs of the people: How they will reduce the burden of poverty, how they will improve power supply, how they will make food and potable water available, how they will provide shelter, improve access to and quality of education, provide community based health insurance for our people and make lives and property more secure.

This strategy of filling our minds with fabricated stories, giving false hope and twisting people's emotional perspectives is limited. At some point, when people see through it as they are bound to, it becomes counter-productive and would backfire. Nothing pays like saying it to the people you are proposing to lead the way it is, no matter how difficult. That is integrity.

The PUNCH
3 March 2015

Why the Yoruba May Lose Out under Buhari

I should make two quick points before I proceed with this. One, I absolutely do not like the ethnic colouration that we give politics in Nigeria. I think that as a country, the best way to attain the height of our potentials is to move together as one, not allowing those things which divide us hold us back.

The second thing, which is a corollary to the foregoing is that I do not support zoning. In truth, I think any government that wants to do Nigeria good should instantly kill the idea of zoning, start to see that every part of the country is fairly treated, gets its due and that people get appointed into offices not because of where they come from but on the strength of their ability. Just give merit the lead and let's see if the sky can hold Nigeria back.

Having said that, it would be playing the ostrich to pretend that I do not understand that the situation with religion and ethnicity will not change in Nigeria overnight. It would not, because whipping those sentiments is currently the most potent weapon in the hands of the political elite and many Nigerians get carried away, following the tide of politicians without question. This is why there have been a lot of permutations about what ethnic group will be influential and which will be redundant in the incoming administration.

One of the often-repeated arguments is that the South-South and South-East have done themselves in by not voting for the All Progressives Congress (APC) thus, jeopardising the opportunity to get any of the juicy political offices under the Buhari administration. Such arguments, steeped in a superior sense of political alertness, are championed by people of Yoruba extraction. A lot of Yoruba-speaking people are so proud of their political leaders and the role they played in the formation of the APC that they write off those who did not join the train as political non-starters with little or no understanding of the times. Depending on who is pushing these arguments and the depth with which they push, I think that they are either naïve or arrogant or are affected by a combination of both.

Of these tendencies, the most unacceptable is arrogance. Unfortunately, it is the most likely in the circumstance even though it is also the most untraditional of the Yoruba. Even if the Yoruba political elite is smart as to be able to read the political barometer and align with the right people at the right time, the traditional Yoruba man does not ordinarily gloat about his achievements. After all, are they not the people who suggest cautious humility when they counsel that if your yam sprouts you should not brag about it? So why beat your own drums so loud despite other ethnic groups?

In this loud vain glory, the Yorubas risk two things. One is that it may dig a deeper gulf between them and the two other zones in the South and two, it may get the North suspicious of the ambition of Yoruba politicians.

Now, we should get this clear, the major, most prominent factor that ensured a Buhari win in the March elections is the long-held determination of the northern part of the country that "power" must return to them in 2015. With due respect to the fact that the South-West delivered votes and more importantly, made it easy for the APC candidate to obtain the required percentage of votes in twenty-five states, northern Nigeria spoke with eloquent unity with their votes during these last elections. The South-West cannot say the same. The zone failed to pull its weight in the measure that bookmakers predicted as total number of votes cast in the zone and those delivered to the APC candidate were incredibly unimpressive. In a zone where over nine million people were said to have collected their permanent voter card before the elections, less than fifty per cent of that number came out to vote. And then out of this number, Buhari got a paltry 2.4 million votes, about 600,000 votes went to President Goodluck Jonathan. Compare this to the North-West where votes from two states, Kano and Jigawa were close to 2.9, almost half a million over the total that the entire South-West offered.

So how does the South-West hope to be equal partners with the North to the extent that its people will disparage other groups in this game? In addition to the side comments referred to earlier, there are reports of the alleged entitled disposition of Senator Bola Tinubu in the distribution of offices as the administration gets closer to forming a government.

This is where the South-West might soon find itself fishing in troubled waters. Yoruba politicians may be smart and strategic, but power is an industry for the North. This is why it sought after the Nigerian presidency with passionate doggedness for years and now that it is in the kitty, they will come against anyone who denies them the opportunity to totally own the president and his administration.

With my understanding of Nigerian politics, politicians from the North are most adept at the deployment of power when one of their own gets into office. I do not see how things would be different when Buhari becomes President especially because of the quantum of support that he got from them. Anyone in doubt should check the political history of Nigeria and see the deal that late eminent Kwara politician, Dr Abubakar Olusola Saraki and late business mogul and politician, Dr Moshood Kashimawo Abiola got from the North in the Second Republic. What leaders of the North, including the political, traditional and religious are likely to do is to move in on Buhari and shield him from any overbearing influence from any other part of the country.

A signal of the political savviness of the North is the success that it allowed the APC - in the North West in particular, and all the three northern zones in general. The result gives credence to the position taken by Professor Ango Abdullahi on behalf of the Northern Elders Forum (NEF) that the North was going to support any party that fields a northern candidate.

With a total of 162 House of Representatives members and forty-six senators from the three zones of the North, it would be easy for the government to get anything done without the help of members from the South-West especially if efforts are made to reach out to lawmakers from the South-East and South-South, most of who belong to the People's Democratic Party (PDP) and already think that the South-West is against their interest. The Yoruba might then just find itself in the cold.

Of course, some would say there is enough consolation in having the vice presidency but between 2003 and 2007, Alhaji Atiku Abubakar had that office without occupying it. Who says that cannot happen again?

This is why Yoruba leaders need to stop flexing muscles now and not overreach themselves. This is why political leaders from this zone must put national interest above the personal, even the regional. This is why the Yorubas must not present themselves as too ambitious in this dispensation. This is why the Yorubas, in spite of whatever advantage, should toe that popular line of seeking equity, justice and the fair treatment of every part of the country. The Yorubas are very well known for that and championing these virtues at the national level is a good way to actualise the promise of change that they made to the people.

Unless this happens, the Yorubas may soon have to contend with a formidable force, which does not just have the capacity for overrun but is prepared to deploy its arsenal to the eternal regret of the group which was the beautiful bride just one day before.

The PUNCH
14 May 2015

Questions Nigerians Should Ask Governors

Most state governors in Nigeria give me a sense that they were elected to merely superintend over the federal allocation accruing to their states. You know, just wait for the monthly Federation Account Allocation Committee (FAAC) meeting to decide the amount due to their states and disburse same as they deem appropriate for every particular month. After which they wait until the next cycle for a repeat.

If governance was all about that, even the neighbourhood carpenter would run a state without a hitch. Or what is the big deal about money dropping on your laps every month and you just having to decide which of your numerous needs to satisfy? That seems pretty easy to me but that is the vibe I get from the level of development in our states.

I think Nigerians allow state governors to easily get away with the lack of creativity at that level of governance. We simply do not take our governors to task. For starters, state and local governments are not just the closest tiers of government in the federal system, the 1999 Constitution also dumps some of the most critical developmental responsibilities on them. Primary and secondary education; primary and secondary healthcare delivery; rural development and such important interventions, aimed at improving the lives of the common man are direct duties of the local and state governments. However, we only just mention local governments here since the joint account structure, which operates between states and the third tier of government has castrated local government administration making them mere adjuncts of the states.

Effectively therefore, there are only two tiers of government in Nigeria, the federal and the state. This makes the state government liable for the improvement of living conditions for the common man within his area and lay the foundation for the future of their children through solid primary and secondary education. The state governments are even able to create employment opportunities for at least a sizeable number of youths in their states. But governors sermonise about how they would love to do these but are handicapped by the dishonesty of managers of the national economy as well as the unpredictable nature of crude oil. Understandably, revenue from crude oil constitutes about 70% of the revenue that goes into the federation account that we all feed on.

Tales from the states have more recently become increasingly woeful. Two weeks ago, Governor Rotimi Amaechi of Rivers state let an audience of which I was part into the financial situation of states. Using his own state as example, the governor said that there was an enormous shortfall in the monetary allocation to the states lately. While his state used to get monthly allocations of over N20b in the past, it has only received a little over N12b in the past few months. As a result, the state is unable to do much since wages take over N9b out of the N12b. He went ahead to reveal that a lot of his colleagues now owe staff salaries and that things were not well with the country.

The Rivers state helmsman who is chair of one of the factions of Nigerian Governors Forum is correct. Although his position poses another agitating question; how is it that state governors who mostly tele-guide national assembly members from their states, find it impossible to mobilise for the passage of the Petroleum Industry Bill and impose some sanity in the oil and gas sector?

Listening to Amaechi that evening, I could not stop wondering whether governors in Nigeria envision states that would ever be independent of handouts from the federation accounts as it happens in other federations. I wondered if they ever looked forward to a moment when a shortfall or total non-availability of these handouts would not lead to the non-payment of workers' salaries.

I wondered if the unpredictable nature of handouts from Abuja would continue to deny Nigerians access to quality and affordable basic education and whether healthcare delivery will forever remain a mirage on account of dwindling resources?

As much as I sympathise with the situations our governors find themselves, they do not need to continue with this helpless attitude. Our governors need a little bit more creative will power to make life better for their people. Just as it was in the 1950s before the discovery of oil, governors must begin to work towards economically viable states even as they campaign for fiscal federalism.

Take a look at the state of California which hosts Hollywood in the United States. Entertainment—from which 6,600 businesses are said to have emerged by simply servicing the filmmaking and television industries—and agriculture are two of the sectors that make California the eighth largest economy in the world.

In spite of the natural endowment of about seventy-four million hectares of fertile land and a wide range of climate variations which allows the production of a variety of food and cash crops, very few states in Nigeria have considered the option of commercial agriculture as a means of revenue generation. This is despite the clear advantages that the venture holds for the country. For example, the invitation extended by the Dr. Bukola Saraki administration in Kwara state to white Zimbabwean farmers to Shonga in 2004 has started to yield results. The farm which is said to employ between 3,000 and 4,000 people every harvest season, produces 2,500 processed frozen chicken daily. The poultry farm is also reported to supply chicken to the fast food company, KFC, even as raw materials from the farms have drawn a lot of investments to the state thereby creating thousands of employment opportunities.

Kwara state again presents an example in healthcare delivery with the introduction of a Community Health Insurance Scheme in the Edu Local government Area in 2007. This scheme—in partnership with the Dutch Health Insurance Fund, Hygeia Community Health and PharmAccess Foundation—allowed individuals yearly registrations with designated medical facilities for two hundred naira. Although the premium has currently increased to five hundred naira, citizens in ten out of the sixteen local governments in the state now benefit from the scheme. The incumbent Governor AbdulFatah Ahmed administration says it aims at achieving universal coverage of the estimated one million rural dwellers in the state by 2018.

While state governors are ever ready to embark on health trips abroad, not one state has thought of exploring health tourism as a means of revenue generation. Yet, states wallow in poverty.

More frightening is the appalling standard of education in the country. While it is right to worry about the state of tertiary education, what should concern us most, in my opinion is that standard of education at the primary and secondary levels, both under the purview of states. On the surface, it looks like a lot of attention is being paid to this level of education especially with the construction of ultra-modern facilities by some states, but state governments need to do far more than this to improve the standard of education. States must take a critical look at the quality of teaching and consider reforms in teacher training. Unless prompt and adequate measures are taken to invest in the quality of teaching that students receive, those fancy buildings will soon succumb to our legendary lack of maintenance tradition.

As 2015 approaches, anyone who becomes governor must be ready to take his state beyond the limitations created by dwindling oil revenue and work for the interest of the people. It is okay for governors to construct flyovers and six-lane roads in state capitals, but they must consider access roads to the villages. As they build luxury government lodges and acquire the most exquisite furnishing on the planet, they must provide quality education for the children of the poor and make healthcare available to everyone. No one elected as governor should continue to lay the blame for non-performance at the feet of Abuja.

The PUNCH
31 October 2014

PART FOUR

Buhari and the Demon of Miscommunication

President Muhammadu Buhari is deficient in so many things, but I do not imagine compassion for Nigerians is one of those. Just think about it, the major reason PMB went against every economic and common-sense counsel to immediately remove subsidy on petroleum products at his ascendancy was for the effect that it would have on the common man. He was said to have insisted that it would engender inflation and that Nigerians will suffer from high costs of essentials. Nice populist argument, if you ask me, even if not a sound economic attitude, especially as the inaction of government is breeding the same inflationary trend that we feared. But I digress.

My point is that the president has, on more than one occasion, radiated a disposition to reason on behalf of the people.

Although the main plank of his unyielding stance on capital control is the one-track nature of the Nigerian economy, I have also heard arguments about how devaluing the Naira will ultimately lead to inflation and hurt the common man.

All of these suggest that the interest of the masses, who defied the elements to cast and monitor their votes was paramount to the president, except that he has not really, personally communicated any of these. And when he communicates, he leaves impressions totally disparate from his man-of the-people image.

Take Buhari's reaction to questions on the restriction of access to foreign exchange by parents who have children schooling abroad during his interview on "Talk To Al Jazeera". The president cut the image of an uncaring leader when he owned up to being wealthy enough to have his children in institutions outside the country but agreed that it was tough luck for Nigerians who would suddenly find themselves unable to cope with the demands of funding the education of their children. Such faux pas are examples of career-defining blunders that leaders make when they do not take communications as seriously as other elements of their jobs.

And in the case of the Nigerian president, evidence abound that neither him nor the totality of his administration understand the essence of effective communication in the administration of nations. It starts with the fact that the president has made the most definitive comments about his government, at one time or the other, when he is outside the country. For example, while Nigerians worried about the delay in the formation of a cabinet, Buhari ignored them and waited until his trip to the United States of America to hint about his plans. He was also out of the country when he revealed that some alleged looters were already returning monies.

President Buhari does not stop at making policy statements while speaking at international forums; he has also made a habit of talking down on Nigerians, sometimes conceding that his people deserve the discriminatory treatments they get outside the country. On occasions, like his latest interview on "Talk with Aljazeera", the president betrayed his disdain for the democratic rights of people to protest when he flatly dismissed the right of the agitators for the new state of Biafra and insisted that he had no reason to dialogue with them no matter what their grouses were.

He is justifiably irate, possibly nauseated by the level of indiscipline in the country, but as the chief marketing officer for the country, he should not say anything other than the positive, which in fact abounds, about the country. How many other presidents so publicly glorify the negative things about their homeland even though there is no country without the burden of deviants? What the President sees as honesty could actually be red flags to foreigners.

It is in this same government that you will have a cacophony of opinions on one single issue. While the very vocal information minister, Alhaji Lai Mohammed would say one thing about the administration's pledge to initiate a welfare package of N5, 000 for unemployed graduates, the president would say another thing. When Mr Mohammed would insist that there was no evidence of padding in the proposed 2016 budget, the president would swear of the inconceivable manipulation inherent in the same budget.

Two weeks after Senior Special Assistant to the President on Media and Publicity, Mallam Garba Shehu said that the country had turned down the membership of the Coalition of Muslim Countries against terrorism; the president would conclusively say that the country would be joining the coalition, even without any engagement with the Nigerian people. He even described those who protest this association as bigots.

This is a government that allows issues drag on thereby allowing speculations and the appropriation of the initiative by forces opposed to the essence of the administration. Take the current state of the economy for instance, the administration has told so much of the problems without explaining, to those who elected it, what it is doing to salvage the situation.

It is not a government interested in the first mover advantage in which it could set the agenda and prevent critics and adversaries from setting the narrative in motion and winning the people to their side. Most often, the president's body language, para-verbal communication and personal space seem to give Nigerians the middle finger. He just does not seem to care what we think.

But when people expect their leaders to step up to issues, they need to act. And that is not just about speed, it is about tempo, a consistent ability to act timely and effectively. And that is nothing more than the ability to efficiently engage stakeholders promptly and through multiple ways.

Unfortunately, even the president's spokespersons are as at sea as himself in the business of communication. Like most Nigerian leaders before him, President Buhari equated success in journalism to effective communication. How erroneous and potentially fatal to the reputation of leaders?

This is why Femi Adesina, Special Adviser to the president on Media and Publicity would, accuse Nigerians—the employers of both his principal and himself—of desiring magic over change. Wouldn't taking time to explain the situation and seeking the understanding of Nigerians, as many times as the occasion demands, send totally different sensations?

Fortunately, it is just the dawn of day for this administration. Fortunately, communications is a skill which can be learned. PMB needs to wean himself of the complex that he is able to save Nigeria by himself. The world is definitely not expecting another messiah and countries only succeed with the active collaboration of every sector of that society, most especially the people.

Rather than alienate any segment of the country through name calling and derogatory remarks, the president should be more receptive. In addressing Nigerians, even when he must be firm, Buhari must understand the importance of humility and the need to promptly tell it all to the people, to explain what is being done about situations and let them know when victory is achieved. He needs to refrain from those international interviews, I plead. PMB should realise that journalists do their homework before interviewing people and his reiteration of the depth of information the Aljazeera host has on the Nigerian budget over him is no display of forthrightness as he may imagine. And his visible irritation at probing questions is no show of strength at all.

Even if he thinks that he needs the whole of his four-year tenure to lay the background for the development of the country, communicating with Nigerians and getting their buy-in should be an essential part of the deal. While at that, he should deny himself the temptation to adopt that personal pronoun "I" and make Nigerians feel more part of the process by employing "we" and "you" in his conversations.

Losing the communication momentum is eroding the reputation, love and trust of the people on which he rode into office. It is a prospect that wisdom should make the president dread like plague.

The PUNCH
10 March 2016

Buhari and the Drums of War in the East

The most debilitating of evils beset men and nations in the exultance that trails their periods of victory. The joy of the exploit of such moments, expose people who do not employ wisdom to two ultimately destructive tendencies.

The first is that they forget where they are coming from, the mistakes that they made yesterday and the weight of repercussions that they suffered from those errors. They move on without any lessons learnt and dap themselves in revelries of their new, if you like, hard won victory. They lose their guard, let their hair down and get vulnerable. In addition, men, when they get the upper hand, momentarily get busy with what they consider to be the important things without attending to the little things. Unfortunately, when such little things are ignored, they gain space; they fester and like little foxes which spoil the vine, little things, when ignored, congregate to destroy the essence of men and nations, unless heed is expeditiously taken.

This is the light in which I see the Federal Government of Nigeria's handling of recent agitations led by the Movement for the Actualisation of Sovereign State of Biafra (MASSOB) and the Indigenous People of Biafra (IPOB). The protests, which have now been suspend followed the arrest and continuous detention of

London, based Nnamdi Kanu. Kanu, Director of Radio Biafra, a propaganda organ for the actualisation of the state of Biafra in reaction to what they refer to as the marginalisation of the south eastern part of the country, was arrested in Lagos on 14 October 2015 shortly after he arrived the country from his UK base. Reports indicate that an Abuja Chief Magistrate Court granted him bail a few days after this but the Department of State Securities (DSS) refused to release him.

To legalise its continuous hold on "the mantle carrier" as some of his supporters call him, the DSS quickly approached the Federal High Court sitting in Abuja for an ex parte order to keep Kanu in detention for ninety days pending investigations.

So Kanu has been in custody for close to sixty days, he has not been allowed to enjoy the bail reportedly granted him by the Magistrate Court even as the case against him is going at snail speed as is customary with lawsuits in Nigeria.

In reaction to his plight, MASSOB and IPOB mobilised for protests in states in the South-East and South-South. They have recorded surprising successes, and on some occasions, these otherwise peaceful protests turned violent with innocent citizens suffering untold hardships. You then wonder the wisdom behind government's handling of Mr Kanu and his Radio Biafra?

Before July 2015 for example, very little was known about Radio Biafra and its proprietor. Although the frequency had been in the news on occasions in the past two years, it did not appear that anyone paid much attention to it until the National Broadcasting Corporation claimed to have successfully jammed its signals. The immediate past Permanent Secretary in the

Federal Minister of Information, Ms Yemi-Esan made the assertion as she left a meeting where she briefed President Mohammadu Buhari on activities of her ministry. It was therefore, not difficult to assume that the declaration had the seal of the president. Unfortunately, Radio Biafra continued with its programming hours after the claim by the federal government. And things have never remained the same. The hitherto unknown radio gained global attention and more listenership in the eastern part of Nigeria where it daily spewed propaganda against the government of the country. Announcing the attempt to stop Radio Biafra from broadcasting was the first misstep of the government in my opinion, as the failure of the attempt unwittingly validated the platform.

In addition, granted that Kanu, from available reports, broadcasts a lot of falsehood and bile about Nigeria—which he is alleged to refer to as a zoo—government made no attempt to attenuate the damage caused for the months. And Kanu, a young man who may have desired nothing more than the federal government's attention is having his time in the sun. Now Kanu's mission has gained traction with media organisations all over the world. He has also gained more supporters in the past few weeks than he garnered in 24 months! The administration has simply provided free publicity services from Kanu and the Biafra idea.

And this brings recollections of the trajectory of the deadly organisation that is now known as Boko Haram. First the Jama'atu Ahlis Sunna Lidda'awati wal-Jihad, as Boko Haram was known then, was neglected and treated with kids' gloves until the uprising between the organisation and security forces in 2009 reportedly left about 1000 people dead. And then the leader,

Mohammed Yusuf mysteriously died in police custody. He was believed to have been summarily executed and Nigeria has never been the same.

Unfortunately, people hardly learn from history. If they did, government would not treat the current agitations with the kind of threats that we have had from the army as well as the police in the past couple of weeks. And now, Kanu's arrest, has suddenly made him a cult hero amongst the people who possibly always shared his sentiment but not his ideology.

The wisdom I thought Nigeria would gain from Boko Haram's gradual decent into annihilative mode is to attend to citizens' discontent with the passion of a father. This is more so because the cry for marginalisation and threats of repercussions is not peculiar to any one ethnic group. Just four years ago, we had some people from the North threatening to make the country ungovernable.

And in the case of PMB, the Igbo nation really does have reasons to worry about a president who once indicated that people who did not vote for him were not likely to get as much of his attention as those who voted for him. They knew that the gauntlet was theirs to take up. This is why Buhari has to go the extra mile to ensure that all ethnic groups in Nigeria are fairly treated.

But in consonance with our tentative attitude to issues, Nigerians, have after the success of the 2015 elections forgotten the much-advertised United States advisory on the dangers that Nigeria might become a failed state in 2015. A 2012 report by some experts on Sub-saharan Africa, who came together under the auspices of America's National Intelligence Council (NIC) suggested that:

… The most important would be the outright collapse of Nigeria. While currently, Nigeria's leaders are locked in a bad marriage that all dislike but dare not leave, there are possibilities that could disrupt the precarious equilibrium in Abuja... Indeed, an overwhelming majority of terrorism in Africa will be caused by indigenous groups waging war against their own or neighbouring governments or against other population groups, defined by religion or ethnicity.

As if oblivious of this scenario painting, Nigerian leaders have, in the wake of the success of the last elections, retreated into their ethnic and religious cocoons, promoting primordial interest and only mouthing national concern.

While President Buhari is pursuing his interest in fighting corruption and setting Nigeria back on the path of sustainable growth as he has promised, one equally important pole of his reform should be resolving the national question. And forestalling insurgencies like the one that has ravaged the north eastern part of the country for the better part of the last decade should be priority. Employing a sledgehammer to crush demands for self-determination as the Biafra situation currently presents would only exacerbate the situation. A country should listen to the grievances of its people and ensure that their children are able to go to school, that their roads and bridges are built, that the best is made of their natural and human resources and that they are seen to be fairly treated in the scheme of things. This appears to be the only way to save Nigeria from being plunged into another insurgency, one which would be too much for it to endure.

The PUNCH
10 December 2015

Goodluck Jonathan: A President for the Season

As a firm believer in the concept of seasons and purpose, I am totally ecstatic about the place Nigeria is today. In a discussion I had last Sunday, one day after Nigeria's most anticipated presidential elections, I said that we were at the threshold of what may be the country's most glorious or most catastrophic moment. And that the way we go would be largely determined by the reaction of politicians and their supporters to the outcome of the previous day's elections.

If you happened to have followed the evolution of Nigeria in the past couple of years, you will understand what I meant. Following a scenario painting by some Americans in 2005, rumours became rife that Nigeria was bound to fail by 2015. These experts on Sub-saharan Africa under the auspices of America's National Intelligence Council noted that Nigerian leaders were "locked in a bad marriage that all dislike but dare not leave" and that the bubble may burst in 2015. This set the stage for utter fear of the approach of 2015 especially as analysts presented the scenario like it was a sacrosanct prediction.

Incidentally, event rolled upon event to help sustain the theory that there might be trouble in 2015. Although the country has had the *Jamā'atu Ahli is-Sunnah lid-Da'wati wal-Jihād,* otherwise known as Boko Haram to cope with since about 2002, for example, it got to a head after the 2011 elections.

Records have it that not less than five thousand civilians were killed by the insurgent between 2009 and 2014. Another one thousand persons have been killed just this year. As of January, thirteen local governments spread between Borno, Adamawa and Yobe states were effectively under the control of the insurgents. The group has also kidnapped hundreds of Nigerians, including girl-children picked from their school premises in Chibok, Borno state about twelve months ago.

In addition to this, leaders of ethnic groups in Nigeria have, since 2011, continually issued threats on the dreadful implications of not having one of their own as president in 2015. Specifically, the Northern Elders Forum (NEF) insisted that the North must have another shot at the presidency while various organisations from the South-South where incumbent President Goodluck Jonathan hails from would not compromise the chance that their son must do another term of four years. So, the die was cast with each group dishing out a measure of threat as repercussion for failure to do their bidding.

Politicians on both major divides also danced to this tune. By the end of January this year, the National Human Rights Commission said that about sixty people lost their lives to pre-election violence in Nigeria. Violence and threats of violence permeated the land, and everyone associated with Nigeria worried that Nigeria would be up in flames after elections.

To drive home this point, a peace agreement was signed in Abuja under the supervision of former Secretary General of the United Nations, Mr Kofi Annan, and former Secretary General of the Commonwealth of

Nations, Chief Emeka Anyaoku in January. That same month, American Secretary of State, Mr John Kerry conferred with major political actors in the country on the need for peaceful, free and fair elections. President Barack Obama was to back this up with an address to Nigeria.

So, the world feared that the worst could happen to Nigeria and everyone was on edge as we went to the polls on Saturday, 28 March 2015. A lot of our compatriots fled the country in anticipation of war even as those who stayed behind remained on the tether, gripped by fear that elections might be manipulated and result in violence that could tear the country apart. All these expectations were based on earlier mentioned threats and the experience of former President Olusegun Obasanjo leading the People's Democratic Party (PDP) on a series of "win by all means elections." But when Obasanjo handed over to late President Umaru Yar A'dua in 2007, Nigeria did not have this measure of pressure towards 2015, it was therefore a different season in the history of the nation, and we needed a leader made for that season.

Enter Goodluck Ebele Jonathan, a non-assuming teacher turned politician who took over Nigeria's presidency after Yar'Adua's death. Carrying on the legacy of his predecessor, Jonathan promised to promote the rule of law as well as reform the electoral process, a fall-out of the guilt feeling they both had about the elections that brought them to power.

The first sign that Jonathan would keep his word was the appointment of Professor Attaihiru Jega as Chairman of the Independent National Electoral Commission (INEC) in June 2010. If you think the appointment of Jega was a non-issue, imagine what would have happened if Jonathan appointed, a pharmacist like Prof Maurice Iwu instead of a first-class political scientist and outstanding man of principle.

Jonathan is said to have given total support to INEC and its chairman in the past five years. Reports say he never queried any innovation proposed by Jega, including the card reader which has finally broken the back of dubious politicians who thrived on multiple voting. Jega also had the free hand to organise staggered elections in five states out of which Jonathan's PDP won only one.

With the enormous power at the disposal of any occupant of Nigeria's presidency, one of the things that people hold against Jonathan is that he did not use the presidency to the advantage of himself and his party. But he seems to be a man who thought more about the collective good. Take the postponement of the elections by six weeks for instance. Although it was suspect at the outset, everyone, including INEC eventually agreed that it was helpful in one way or the other. However, within those six weeks, a myriad of speculations aimed at either preempting Jonathan or just further tarnishing his reputation flew around. He was said to nurse the idea of an interim government, some swore that elections would not hold, others said that he planned to handover to the military as a measure of how much he hated General Mohammadu Buhari. Added to the foregoing, were vociferous agitations for the removal of Jega on the strength of various accusations of bias and support for the opposition.

Some people would suggest that none of these is possible in a democracy but anyone familiar with the dictatorial tendencies of many pseudo-democrats in Africa know that a desperate leader could go ahead and play out one or more of these options for self-preservation, without any care that he might plunge his country into crisis. Yet, Jonathan kept assuring that he would not allow any of these to happen. The presidential elections held on March 28 and the whole world waited in anxiety for the unfolding of Nigerian's Armageddon, which was expected to unfold during the revelation of the winner of the elections.

As it became apparent that Jonathan and his PDP were losing the elections, many Nigerians were gripped with fear considering the threat of war by Jonathan's kinsmen. Disturbed by this prospect like other Nigerians, I prayed as I wrote in a letter to the president on this page two weeks ago, that he would find the grace to accept the election result and step further to congratulate General Mohammadu Buhari, something that no Nigerian leader has ever done.

Jonathan found the grace as at about 5:15 p.m. on Tuesday. He put a call across to the president-elect, congratulated him and assured him of his cooperation. It was one noble move which shocked everyone including the General Abdusalam Abubakar, chairman of the National Peace Committee on 2015 Presidential Election. Jonathan later released a statement in which he reiterated his determination to entrench free and fair elections and his conviction that his ambition was not worth the blood of any Nigerian.

So, while Nigerians cannot agree on how much Jonathan achieved in the five years that he led Nigeria, delivering credible elections in which he conceded defeat to the opposition party, setting Nigeria on an incredible path to democratic growth, is an achievement worthy of celebration. This could as well be the purpose for which God has sent Jonathan to us at this time and I dare say, this man has fulfilled that purpose and history will never forget him.

The PUNCH
2 April 2015

History Will Judge Jonathan and Buhari

Finally, the 2015 general elections are upon us. Arguably the most anticipated elections in the recent history of Nigeria, expectations and rumours of war concerning 2015 started early. For nearly one decade, political analysts in Nigeria have claimed that the Central Intelligence Agency (CIA) predicted that this year would be Nigeria's Armageddon, in spite of repeated denials by the United States government. The prophecy of doom has acquired a life of its own with people all over world anxious that Nigeria might implode and self-destruct this year.

A report published in *THISDAY* on 15 May 2012 clarified that what was erroneously referred to as predictions that Nigeria will be a failed state by 2015 was a mere scenario painting by some experts on Sub-saharan Africa, who came together under the auspices of America's National Intelligence Council (NIC) to discuss likely trends in the region over the next fifteen years from January 2005. To drive home the non-involvement of the United States in any opinion held by these experts, the NIC was said to have issued a disclaimer on the first page of the report saying: "The views expressed are those of individuals and do not represent official US intelligence or policy positions."

One of the views expressed in the seventeen-page document entitled: "Mapping Sub-Saharan Africa's Future" is as follows:

> Other potential developments might accelerate decline in Africa and reduce even our limited optimism. The most important would be the outright collapse of Nigeria. While currently Nigeria's leaders are locked in a bad marriage that all dislike but dare not leave, there are possibilities that could disrupt the precarious equilibrium in Abuja. The most important would be a junior officer coup that could destabilise the country to the extent that open warfare breaks out in many places in a sustained manner.

The report, which is based on a lot of conjecture, then warned:

> If Nigeria were to become a failed state, it could drag down a large part of the West African region. Even state failure in small countries such as Liberia has the effect of destabilising entire neighbourhoods. If millions were to flee a collapsed Nigeria, the surrounding countries, up to and including Ghana, would be destabilised. Further, a failed Nigeria probably could not be reconstituted for many years if ever and not without massive international assistance…

However, there is no denying the fact that these are very worrisome times. The stakes for the 2015 elections are just so high with every part of the country holding on to positions which do not help the survival of the country.

For instance, northern Nigeria has made no secret of its boredom with not occupying the number one position in the land and maybe justifiably so. But for the unfortunate death of late President Umaru Musa Yar'Adua barely two years after his swearing, a Nigerian of northern descent would just have been concluding his second term this May. But Yar'Adua's transition put paid to what would have been a perfect rotational arrangement as his erstwhile deputy, Goodluck Jonathan was sworn in as President. Jonathan then went on to contest and win the 2011 elections, something that those who speak for the North did not find funny.

The result is that Jonathan cannot be said to have ever had the support of some leaders of the North. Not even in the fight against the dreaded Boko Haram insurgents does the president have the support of groups like the Northern Elders Forum (NEF). The NEF did not only see the declaration of state of emergency in the three north-eastern state mostly affected by the insurgency as a declaration of war on the North, it also threatened to drag the immediate past army chief to the International Criminal of Justice (IJC) for war crimes.

Then there is the unhelpful posture of some of Jonathan's Ijaw and Niger Delta kinsmen. Recently, leader of the Niger Delta Peoples Volunteer Force, (NDPVF), Alhaji Mujahid Asari-Dokubo and a former militant leader, High Chief Government Ekpemupolo, alias Tompolo were reported to have vowed to unleash war on the country in the event that Jonathan loses the upcoming presidential elections. Although Jonathan's Special Adviser on the Niger Delta, Mr Kingsley Kuku has said that reports of alleged threat to national security by these men were not accurate, the president's people are desperate to have him back in office after the elections.

Nigeria also has politicians who left the ruling People's Democratic Party(PDP) to join and give bite to the chances of the opposition All Progressive Congress (APC) to deal with in the upcoming elections, among these is Rivers state governor and director general of the Muhammudu Buhari Campaign Organisation, Mr Rotimi Amaechi is the most outspoken, nothing but the trouncing of Jonathan at these elections would be adequate pay back for forcing them out of the PDP after they helped him get into office in 2011.

Amaechi, although a beneficiary of the powers of the judiciary in a spectacular way, has therefore gone from giving tacit approval to mutinies in the Nigerian Army to threatening that his party would form a parallel government if rigged out in the coming elections.

Then, the seeming sloppy preparation of the Professor Attahiru Jega led Independent Electoral Commission (INEC) which is giving Nigerians sleepless nights. When we juxtapose all of this with another aspect of the 2005 NIC report which addressed terrorism, we would find dismissing the report a bit more perilous. According to the report:

Given that significant portions of Africa, those areas outside the nation's capitals, will essentially be ungoverned, there will be many opportunities for terrorist groups that threaten the West to seek haven across the continent...those terrorists groups seeking sanctuary for their fugitive principals or who want to hide dangerous weapons may find the distant regions of some African countries inviting precisely because they are unlikely to be interrupted by government…Indeed, an overwhelming majority of terrorism in Africa will be caused by indigenous groups waging war against their own or neighbouring governments or against other population groups, defined by religion or ethnicity.

Now, the accuracy of the foregoing is without question, a reason for which political leaders in Nigeria must put national interest ahead of party, ethnic and other primordial considerations. Despite the gloomy prognosis staring us in the face, I am confident that Nigeria is able to make unqualified success of these elections and go one to prove that the country is ready to move on in the long journey toward democratic governance.

To save Nigeria and the world the unrest that violence after the elections portends, President Jonathan must rededicate himself to the promise of electoral justice that he made to Nigerians. His administration must not compromise the integrity of our security forces by recruiting them to intimidate political opponents or work in favour of the ruling party. And if the president loses, he must brace up for it, accept the judgment of Nigerians in good faith and work with the winner to move the country forward. He must also prevail on all his supporters to maintain the peace and not turn the nation into a war zone because of his loss. If he wins, he must be magnanimous in victory and warn his supporters not to gloat about it.

Same goes for General Buhari. A win should come with magnanimity. And if he thinks he has lost unfairly, his first reaction to the results would determine the response of his supporters. Buhari must have confidence in the ability of the Nigerian judiciary to redress any electoral injustice and prevail on his supporters to perish the idea of a parallel government or any form of civil disobedience.

No matter how the 2015 presidential election goes, the history of democracy in Nigeria would not be complete without the names of Jonathan, Buhari and Jega prominently mentioned. Time will reveal which of these names will be written in glory and which will be written in ignominy. But it is a choice available for the individual to make now!

The PUNCH
5 February 2015

Shiite Crisis: Nigeria is Playing with Fire

No matter what the Nigerian Army and the Nigeria Police Force say in the aftermath of the latest face-off with members of the Islamic Movement of Nigeria, this country cannot justify the measure of force its agents have continued to unleash on this religious group. But this incident, in which an unclarified number of people lost their lives, is indicative of the precarious security situation the country is in as well as the questionable proactive conflict resolution credentials of Nigerian leaders. We shall return to this reality presently.

For three days this last week, the otherwise peaceful atmosphere of the Federal Capital Territory, Abuja, has been disrupted by violent clashes between the men of the army and members of the IMN with numbers of causalities ranging from three to fifty depending on who you are speaking with. No matter what account you have, the incentive for this crisis is the fundamental distrust between the government, its agencies and the Shiites. This distrust is immediately attributable to the December 2015 clash between the army and members of the sect. At the end of the series of events, which saw the army advance on the sect in what looked like a retaliatory action, over three hundred people including men and women had been killed.

But it did not stop at that. Leader of the sect, Sheik Ibrahim El-Zakzaky, was subsequently arrested with his wife, and the two have been in what authorities call protective custody despite court orders for their release for almost two years. Members of the sect have continued to agitate for the release of their leader, while the Buhari government has kept him like its survival depends on it. To some extent, the mutual distrust between the two parties accounts for the frequent clashes that occur. While law enforcement agencies understandably expect the sect to approach it for protection before embarking on processions like the ones that precipitated the recent skirmishes, the sect has, with government's defiance of court orders for the release of their leaders, already assume a no-love lost situation with the authorities; and there, you have a recipe for an unending confrontation.

But Nigeria would be the bigger loser at the end of the day. True, the religious sect is likely to continue to lose its members, but those are precious Nigerian lives that are illegally killed by the country that should protect them. Therefore, Nigeria would not just be decimating its own human capital, it would also be alienating itself from the civilised world; thereby, accentuating its poor leadership. What is more frightening is the IMN's tendency to go underground and start a guerrilla warfare before long. This was pretty much the trajectory of the Jama'atu Ahlis Sunna Lidda'awatiwal-Jihad before it became the Boko Haram group. A group to which Nigeria has lost at least twenty thousand lives, with about two million people displaced and an estimated five million facing severe food shortages. How much of this type of internal strife a country can bear is best left to imagination given the quantum of conflicts that Nigerian security agencies currently deal with. For the record, none of the six geopolitical zones of the country is conflict-free at the moment. While the North-West is dealing with the issues of banditry and religious conflicts like the one from which seventy people were killed in Kaduna state penultimate week, the North-East is under the terror of the Boko Haram insurgency while the North-Central is engulfed in daily scuffles between marauding herdsmen and farmers. Thousands of lives have also been lost on these turfs. And apart from the appalling loss of lives in the latter case, it bears a frightening indication of the food crisis that the country might end up with in no distant time.

Down South, Nigeria is grappling with temperamental militants holding the country at the jugular in the Niger Delta region, the incessant mumbles of agitations for self-determination in the South-East by the IPOB agitators as well as the multiple crimes of cultism, kidnappings and political violence in the South-West. That is not to speak of the alarming volume of small arms and light weapons that have found their way into the country or the unchecked access to psychotropic drugs amongst Nigerians especially the youths. The authorities have no answer to most of these challenges other than the deployment of troops, numbers, strength and capacity of which are indeed not inexhaustible.

Speaking at the second annual conference of the Guild of Corporate Online Publishers recently, former chairman of the National Human Rights Commission, Prof. Chidi Odinkalu, sounded the alarm on Nigeria. He quoted from a lecture delivered by the Minister of

Interior, Abdurahman Dambazzu, at the National Defence College in June 2018 as follows:

The nature and extent of internal security in Nigeria have therefore been redefined by the various emerging threats which are far more serious and difficult for the Nigerian Police to handle… the role of the armed forces has equally been redefined by this same situation. The role of the Nigerian Armed Forces in internal security seems to have gone beyond providing military aid to civil authority (otherwise known as MACA) or to civil power (MACP). The armed forces seem to be now spearheading all internal security operations due to the fact that the Nigeria Police is no longer in a position to handle such matters effectively. What we are dealing with currently is tilted more towards low-intensity conflicts and/or asymmetric warfare, which is within the purview of military operations other than war (MOOTW).

If the interior minister was this point-blank about the security challenges that the country faces and the inefficiencies that exist in the security architecture, expectations would be that leaders of the country should be deliberate about reducing the areas of conflict. This is not just because the country's military are nearly stretched out of its limits by duties that do not constitutionally belong to them but more so because there really can be no development in a country with the various levels of conflicts that Nigeria is dealing with.

Following the uncertainties attending these conflicts are the disruptions in economic activities and the erosion of public confidence in the ability of government to guarantee the security of lives and property. The Nigerian government seems to have reached a conclusion that these can only be achieved by force; but how much has that achieved so far? Now, it has not only failed to achieve the foregoing, it is unwittingly also worsening the security situation, the productive capacity of the populace and the prospect for new investments.

With the reality that Nigeria will soon be entering a season of elections in which politicians are known to be at their most irresponsible best, the Muhammadu Buhari administration must lead Nigeria on a path to peace. A good place to start is obeying the court order for the release of El-Zakzaky on bail and then commencing multilateral discussions for the resolution of the IMN situation and so many others that do not necessarily call for the display of military valour. And why is it so herculean to empower the Nigeria Police to perform its civic duties? Would equipping the police and training its men to respond to these civil issues not save the country from unnecessary bloodletting perpetrated by the military?

The PUNCH
1 November 2018

PART FIVE

Are We Not All Living in Destitution?

One of the telling signs of Nigeria's undeveloped state is the inability to maintain accurate data about anything and everything. We do not even know our exact population. The other probably sadder thing is the deliberate falsehood we peddle about our situation. We get all defensive and even abusive, we just do not like to see ourselves in the mirror.

Just some weeks back, Mr Festus Odimegwu, then chairman of the Nigerian Population Commission, stirred the hornets' nest when he queried the credibility of past census conducted and warned about the failure lurking in wait for the 2016 exercise. The reaction that greeted the assertion was violent and it did not abate until the poor man was removed from office for nothing other than his failure to be politically correct. His refusal to watch the national mood and realise that there are just some things that should not be said. In the aftermath of his removal, I asked myself if Nigerians did not realise what he revealed. I know he was right, although he also did not say it all. The truth is that every section of Nigeria is guilty of this unfortunate manipulation, the level of ignorance in the country sees to that. Communities do everything to increase their numbers as they believe that it would determine the "goodies" that accrue to them when government eventually looks their way, so what all the fuss about? Sheer hypocrisy!

The most current example of our contempt for the truth is the argument about whether a hundred million Nigerians live in destitution as World Bank Country Director for Nigeria, Marie-Francoise Marie-Nelly, postulated last week. Marie-Nelly, who said this at the bank's Country Programme Portfolio Review in Enugu revealed that the number of Nigerians living in destitution makes up 8.33 per cent of the total number of people living in destitution all over the world. But trust our government never to lie low. The World Bank staffer got a piece of the mind of Nigeria's Federal Government. In a statement issued by Economic Adviser to the President, Dr Nwanze Okidegbe, government boldly refuted the claim.

Among many other things, Okidegbe's stated: "Rather than engage in peddling easily disprovable and inaccurate poverty numbers, we believe it would be better for the World Bank to focus its attention on designing programmes and interventions to support the government's efforts in accelerating poverty reduction in Nigeria." The only thing that came to my mind after reading this statement was to ask the presidential aide to kindly tell us the number of destitute Nigerians since he was so sure that they were not up to 100 million. My bet is that he would never be able to.

How then did he arrive at the conclusion that the statement made by the World Bank staff was untrue? Even if I do not have any way to prove the veracity of the hundred million number, I am sure that it would be closer to reality than any figure that government may brandish. To sustain my gut feeling, I searched for the meaning of "destitution". The definition which appeals to me, according to dictionary.com is the one that describes the word as "deprivation, lack, or absence." Now can we in all conscience say that we do not have more than hundred million Nigerians who are deprived of the good things of life?

How many Nigerians live in humane accommodation for example? How many Nigerians can afford to provide balanced meals for their households? How many Nigerians have access to quality healthcare? What type of transportation do majority of Nigerians travel by? How many of our compatriots can send their children to the schools of their choice? The reality is that the vast majority of Nigerians just manage to get by.

If you have ever visited a General Hospital for instance, you would see the pathetic conditions under which Nigerians are treated. It gets worse if a patient needs to be admitted. Even in Lagos state, patients are admitted and placed on drip on the corridors of hospitals. Sometimes, they are placed on worn out mattresses simply because there are no more beds inside the wards. At other times, they are admitted on benches outside the hospital ward until some patients in the wards are discharged. So, patients are left at the mercy of the elements as well as parasites like mosquitoes and other insects that feast on them. There is no better way to describe destitution. If these Nigerians had a choice, they would be in private hospitals where they would be respected.

The presidential adviser should sound out some of the junior civil servants who work around him. A man who takes home the minimum wage of 18,000 naira would never be able to afford anything near a decent accommodation for example. It is from this meagre sum that he is expected to feed his family, transport himself to work, send his children to school, pay hospital bills and take care of myriads other responsibilities including buying water for the need of his family. Yet, we say this family does not live in destitution. Are we waiting until they die?

Daily, on the streets across Nigerian cities, you see hapless young men and women roaming around in the name of job hunting. These jobs are not there, and government is not ready to do anything for them. Thousands of Nigerians cannot afford meals in their homes, so every now and then, you see very long queues of people fighting to fill their stomachs with some cheap, badly prepared food which exposes them to cholera and typhoid, when most countries of the world have forgotten of such aliments.

As bad as things are, however, no government is thinking of doing anything radical to alleviate the suffering of the masses in Nigeria. Our governments are not thinking about community health insurance for indigent Nigerians, or housing schemes that could make things better for the indigent, or free education. Rather, our government and their agencies are imposing more fines, forcing us to obtain new drivers licenses and car registration at costs that most Nigerians cannot readily afford.

But it does not seem that they even understand how much they are driving the people further into penury—at least Dr. Nwanze Okidegbe does not know. Rather than gloat over achievements that do not trickle down to needy Nigerians, I would expect people in government to reflect over observations like the one made by Marie-Nelly. In case they are under any illusions, government officials should search their souls and execute new collaborations, across arms and tiers of government, that can bring succour to the people. It just does not end with statements which do not speak to our realities because as it currently stands, this country does not just favour the poor.

The PUNCH
29 November 2013

The Church, Tithing and the Rest of Us

I did not think I would join this unending conversation on the propriety of paying tithes until I saw a friend who is not of the Christian faith share a critical article in the past week. That meant two things to me: first being that the church can no longer hide from the scrutiny of the world and the other being that a lot of people, who do not necessarily understand the spiritual essence of some of the doctrines of Christianity also joined in the condemnation.

I find such interloping unacceptable and preposterous. In the same way in which I would not impugn the wisdom in the doctrine that a practising Muslim must visit the Holy City of Mecca in his lifetime or that a worshipper of the Yoruba god of farming must not eat the new yam until he sacrifices unto his deity, I do not expect non-Christians to fault my subscription to the payment of tithes in church. All these gestures, to my understanding, bear deep spiritual undertones, which may make sense to no other person but the one who connects with them. But I also realise that intervening in the rights of people to be what they have chosen to be, even when their choices do not necessarily impede on our own freedom, is a common pastime of the average Nigerian. This is why I query the prospect that democracy, the way the West observes it, will ever work with us. Democracy and democratic principles thrive on the ability to allow a person to be what they desire to be as much as they do not hurt another's interest or trample on the rule of law; rule of law, being the emblem of the state's paternalistic obligation to its citizens. Democracy has, over the years, evolved to become the most apt exemplification of the aphorism: "live and let live".

But that is not our life as a people. Nigerians, no matter how old they are or what status they attain, must still defer to their biological parents and people of their parents' age. The latter group does not even need to be of any close affinity. The passage of years, evidenced by any physical sign, conveys the licence for the aged to guide you and sometimes, insist on what you must and must not do. This is why some politicians become godfathers circumventing the general will, imposing their political decisions on the people and sometimes, maintaining that without their way, there would be no other way. This is the reason why a journalist of the status of Bashorun Dele Momodu would interview a politician that is not in the favour of a vocal set of Nigerians and they do not just condemn him but also query his integrity. It is why a politician becomes evil simply by not associating with a preferred set of people. Nigerians have a standard that they have painted in their minds for everyone and once you don't live by those standards, you are a renegade, regardless of your age, qualification or status in life. I suggest this is a major reason why we will struggle with democracy for a long time to come. But I digress.

Concerning Christianity, my point is that if you do not belong to the faith and do not subscribe to a doctrine, you really should restrain from questioning the right of people to worship in the way they choose.

Having said that, it makes sense to say here that those who profess the Christian faith are manifestly the same people who invite the intervention and sometimes, the pillorying of people outside the faith. At the same time, one should clarify that while it is possible to adjudge such outspoken Christians as unfaithful, such random condemnation would beg the issue. What we should do, when people within our number elect to wash our attire in public glare is to call them aside and interrogate their motivation, which may sometimes, simply border on lack of information.

Experience will show that not every rebellion is borne out of malice. Some indeed emanate from a deep quest for better understanding or for the reform of systems that seem to alienate. And in such instances, reasoning together, rather than returning fire for fire, should be the strategy. But the Church in Nigeria lacks strategy. With due respect, the Church in Nigeria, if there could be anything so addressed in the sense in which the proponents of the idea conceptualised it, is the first enemy of itself.

Principally, an organised body, which is what a church should be, should speak with one voice. It should have a common position on the essential ingredients of the faith and be ready to speak up for the faith every time there is a need to. Most importantly, such a body must be ready to answer questions, raised by adherents. And I dare say, answering such questions should be without regard to motive. The Church should, without minding whether inspiration came from mischievous or altruistic quarters, attend to queries from the faithful, and when need be, from outside the faith, with all joy. After all, Christ, whose prototype the Church is, spoke about and lived for love for all men. It is the failure of the church to treat posers with such childlike affection, which results in the incessant misunderstanding and suspicions that there is more than meets the eye in its operations. And this is another issue that the church must address as a collective. How is it that the entry barrier to ministry in Nigeria is so low? How is it that there is no self-check or regulation, or is it that every jobless man and woman who can afford a Bible becomes a pastor? How is it that there is so much alleged abuse amongst the clergy and the Church is unable to confront and discourage impostors? It is correct to say that there have been forewarnings about deceptions and the manipulations of the people's minds in the name of religion even before the advent of Christianity but that does not preclude self-censorship within the faith; it indeed should encourage the faithful to self-check.

However, not even the absence of such internal regulation detracts from the very constructive roles that faith organisations have played in the development of Nigeria. In reference to the assumptions that have become rife about the lack of accountability in the administration of tithes for instance, a more united and outspoken church would have shown the world that tithes paid into churches are not only deployed into the sustenance of church leaders, but also into the training of millions of under-privileged children, the provision of food, medical treatment, rehabilitation of youths and a myriad of other social ventures whose amplification the conservative nature of the Christian service discourages. That point would have been made without detracting from the need for relative comfort for those called into ministry. The life of a pastor is not just about preaching on Sundays, even though that itself is no mean responsibility. But in addition to that, it is a call unto unending denial signified by sleepless nights spent interceding for others and hours of counselling and tending to the spiritual and other needs of people.

There are claims that people are manipulated into paying tithes, but that is laughable. Even if pastors talk endlessly about the importance of paying tithes to receiving God's blessings, the faithful obey because of their self-interest. Otherwise, how are pastors able to convince people to pay tithes but they cannot stop them from committing all the atrocities that litter around us? Should this also preclude accountability in church affairs? Absolutely not. But then accountability to whom? I do not imagine that anyone who claims to have been called into the service of God and humanity would object to being answerable to anyone who contributes to the purse of his fold. In the same way in which every congregation should, in accordance with the laws of the land, audit their account periodically and prepare same ready for inspection at any time.

Such level of probity should be the default state of the church for that is the only way in which it would remain in the world without necessarily being of the world. In spite of the noise and level of compromises around it, the church must remain the light as was contemplated from the start. That is the only way not to bring the faith into disrepute and affect the world positively in line with the great commission.

The Cable
7 December 2017

Does Life Really Begin at Forty in Nigeria?

Once I listened to Professor Onyebuchi Chukwu, Minister of Health speaking about President Goodluck Jonathan's approval of the Nigeria National Stroke Prevention Programme. According to Chukwu, government developed this programme to encourage people check their health status because it was worried about the alarming rate of sudden death among Nigerians, particularly those in their prime The minister informed of the government's collaboration with federal teaching hospitals and some Nigerians in the Diaspora to bring this programme to Nigerians at the subsidised rate of N10,000. And to lead by examples, Jonathan and his vice, Namadi Sambo submitted themselves for demo tests.

Although it was gladdening that government had noticed the now rampant loss of lives, especially of people in their 40s and 50s, it remains difficult to understand how indigent Nigerians—on whose behalf Chukwu claimed government was spending a N40,000 subsidy—would access this seemingly laudable idea. I thought to myself that government was either playing politics or they were totally ignorant of the widely known fact that close to seventy per cent of Nigerians do not have more than two hundred naira daily. How do such people raise the N10,000 for these health checks? Unless of course, the programme is meant for the privileged thirty per cent and government really has no care for the bulk of poor people in the country. Not surprisingly, three weeks after the initial drama, we have not heard a word from the Federal Ministry of Health on how Nigerians would access this programme, as out of reach of the common man as it is.

However, the Nigerian Medical Association (NMA) brought this all-important issue back to national consciousness at a press conference announcing its Physicians Week. According to NMA National President, Dr Osahon Enabulele, the association will discuss the theme: "Federalism and Nigeria's Healthcare System- an Appraisal of the Primary and Secondary Healthcare System" and the sub-theme "Demystifying Sudden Death in Nigeria- Developing Legislation for Regular Health Check-up in Nigeria," The NMA then called on the: "executive and legislative arms of government at local, state and federal government levels to create a separate day, at least six-monthly or once a year dedicated to free health check-up by Nigerian citizens under their jurisdiction." The association went on to lament the alarming rate at which young Nigerians die and called on governments at all levels to ensure that citizens have access to proper medical attention to increase life expectancy. This has got me thinking about the health risks that Nigerians bear.

As a child, I heard so much about how life beginning at forty that I truly imagined that the first thirty-nine years of life are preparatory to the real thing, but general life expectancy in Nigeria and the actual loss of young people have made me rethink if life truly begins at 40. I understand that this expression was in the reversal of an earlier notion that "death begins at forty." It was said that life expectancy in Mediaeval England was around twenty-five and only reached forty sometime around the turn of the twentieth century when society could offer a measure of affluence that allowed citizens, especially women some respite from the drudgery that characterised preceding eras.

One account claims that the phrase was first inferred in relation to the health of women. An old article in the New York Times pointed out that Mrs Theodore Parsons who was Physical Director of Schools in Chicago wrote a book, *Brain Culture through Scientific Body Building* in 1912 where she spoke about the newly found importance of the age of forty. She was quoted in an article reportedly published in *The Pittsburgh Press* sometime in 1912 as follows: "...Death begins at thirty, that is, deterioration of the muscle cells sets in. Attention to diet and exercise would enable men and women to live a great deal longer than they do today..."

The truth is that the age of forty comes with a lot of baggage as the body gradually begins to make its journey back the way it came. It is like checking out the performance of a brand-new car, five years after we bought it. Each part of the car would have suffered different levels of depreciation and its continued use would demand more than mere routine service. It is the same with our bodies.

By forty, the human body is on a downward slope. This is more so in this side of the world where a lot of forty-year-olds struggle with more vicissitudes of life. Unlike in the days of our fathers, more people in their 40s are raising children as more people have delayed marriages and childbearing. At a stage in which our parents were thinking about consolidation or even retirement, today's forty-year-olds are paying school fees and struggling to make ends meet. The current political climate has also fostered career crashes and unemployment with the result that men and women must continually re-invent themselves, find new directions and make new choices in their lives.

The position in which many forty-year-olds currently finds themselves would unfortunately likely increase the risk of high blood pressure, heart disease and diabetes, which are three of the most common conditions they are susceptible to. The propensity for such afflictions and the complications associated with them is worsened by the poor health infrastructure in our country, the lack of neither adequate health education nor health care delivery, which is why I find the NMA suggestion interesting. It is why I am also thinking that the Nigeria Labour Congress (NLC) and other labour unions should begin to take government up on the provision of affordable healthcare for their members. While Lagos and Kwara have a semblance of community health insurance schemes, other states are playing catch-up. As we continue to hope that government wakes up to its responsibility however, it is important that every Nigerian especially those who are above forty observe an easy-to-maintain wellness plan. Habits which are important to reducing health risks include maintaining an exercise regime; reducing the intake of alcohol and tobacco; limiting the consumption of sweets; cutting down on meat, especially red meat and other fatty foods; eating plenty fruits and vegetables; restricting sodium intake and getting as much rest as possible. Regular medical check-ups for blood pressure, blood sugar level as well as cancers like prostrate, cervical and breast should be part of the routine for everyone above forty.

I guess that part of the wisdom that is attributed to the age of forty is taking your wellbeing into your own hands and deciding to avoid anything which may bring premature death your way. True, the life and death of man is not in his hands but choices about the quality of life that we live are in our hands. I think seeking information about the best choices and making those choices is the wisdom which comes with the age and one sure way to see that life truly begins at forty.

Newsdiary Online
1 November 2013

Does Nigeria Really Have a Future?

For someone who became deaf and blind at nineteen months old, the late American political activist and intellectual, Hellen Keller, stood in a good place to lecture the world about optimism. Years after she defied her handicap to become a political and leading campaigner for women's suffrage, labour rights, socialism and such other interests, Keller offered the world the following words on the idea of optimism: "Optimism is the faith that leads to achievement. Nothing can be done without hope and confidence."

Denied of two of the vital senses that make living meaningful, only a passionately positive attitude could produce the magic that this lady's life turned out to be. Optimism worked for her as it has worked for men and women all through the ages. Yet, this principle, like most others fed by the psychology of men, could be a double-edged sword. For instance, Nigerians are some of the most positive people in the world, yet the country has remained an uninspiring example of what a modern nation state should not be. So, while optimism is a commendable attribute, exercising it without reason and moderation could lead to a potentially harmful denial of reality and pain.

Things are a bit worse in Nigeria because the people's optimism is not necessarily borne out of any obvious strategy to arrive at the future that the people anticipate. Most of the time, the excessive hope expressed by Nigerians is based on some unseen spiritual convictions rather than concrete and infallible proofs of actions that change the fortune of nations. That is not to say that there is anything wrong with being spiritual, but the truth is that religion itself recognises the place of work and reward. Every religion is guided by a set of principles by which its adherents could access the blessings that it promises them, and it would be foolhardy to hope for reward when work has not been done. A good example is the Christian proclamation that salvation is free while that is not exactly so. It is free to the extent that someone had paid for it by shedding his blood ahead for beneficiaries, and that is the same way that great nations are built. The vision of founding fathers and the disciplined sacrifices that they made are the waters of the seeds of greatness that some countries can currently lay claim to. Such vision and discipline are plainly rare on the leadership landscape in Nigeria, so you wonder what the pervasive hope that "it will be better" is anchored on.

Every waking day, Nigeria is reminded of its status as the nation with some of the worst developmental indices anywhere in the world. The country is said to have the highest number of the poorest of the poor in the world. This suggests that the majority of Nigerians are unable to feed three times daily, access affordable and quality healthcare or send their children to schools or aspire for any meaningful future.

Now, the country's disposition to education is particularly worrisome. Every nation aspiring for greatness knows that education, which aids the expansion of the mind and vision of people and grows their capacities to identify right from wrong as well as understand the importance of peace, justice and fairness is an irreducible minimum demand for national development. But no one seems to pay attention to the needs of the nation in this area. But for Governor Nasir el-Rufai of Kaduna state who launched a revolutionary reassessment of the quality of primary education in addition to seeking creative ways of improving the enrolment, retention and completion of basic education by Nigerian children, not much attention is being paid to the about fifteen million children of primary school age who are out of school in the country.

The state of public health and the administration of health in general is as parlous as education such that you wonder how a people who do not care about planning for the education of their children or ensuring that its human capital is in good physical and mental well-being are unbothered; neither do the activities of political leaders in the country suggest a break from these grim circumstances. Starting from the absence of the free atmosphere required for democracy to thrive, the Nigerian political class have turned the nation into an enclave for the achievement of their own selfish ambitions to the neglect of the people they claim to represent. Not even any of the political divides they claim to associate with makes any difference.

The ruling All Progressives Congress has for the best part of the last couple of weeks been involved in multiple level muscle-flexing that has left the people more distraught than happy. The leaders of today are redefining the essence of democracy through their win-by-all-means philosophy which subverts the will of the people and leave those who should work for the progress of the nation struggling for their own interests. Last week re-run of the governorship election in Osun state is a typical example of leadership forcing their will on the people and damning the consequences.

The People's Democratic Party, which has the opposition status, does not present any comforting alternative. Just last week, Rivers state Governor, Nyesom Wike, threw caution to the wind and told the whole world in no uncertain terms that the PDP has remained a party where internal democracy is alien. His insistence on hosting the party's national convention and threats of the fate that would befall the party in the event that the party did not toe his line suggested an ulterior motive that could be of no interest other than his own. Nigerians are therefore left with little or no option than to choose between the hard rock and the deep blue sea.

However, what is most pathetic in all of us is that the people who are at the receiving end of the treachery of the political class are themselves becoming collaborators in the perpetuation of their own suffering. The political class is bereft of ideas that would move the country forward and the people are contended with the crumbs fed them by their oppressors.

While it is the democratic right of every citizen to affiliate with political interests of his choice, a citizenry with the future in mind come together when issues that affect the development of their country is concerned. But not Nigeria. People of this country are too drawn by their partisan interests to come to a consensus about developmental issues. They are mostly star-struck spectators who cheer on their oppressors. You are then forced to wonder where the hope that Nigeria has a glorious future is hinged.

So, here is the truth, as it currently stands, praying, fasting and staying optimistic until thy kingdom come, will leave Nigeria in its state of development. The only prospect for a change is that the people wake up to their reality of the deprivations that binds them together in spite of their political and other affiliations, put the politicians to task and demand a change for the country with all their might.

The PUNCH
4 October 2018

How Precious is Human Life to You, Dear Nigerian?

There are some stories you hear in Nigeria that make your heart bleed and make you wonder if the people of this country are ready to break the shackles of underdevelopment.

While we are all quick to identify the speck in the eyes of others, especially our leaders, we refuse to acknowledge, not to speak of removing the log in our own eyes. We forget that the values – moral and ethical composition of a people – define the present and future of such a people.

Most often than not, we attribute all the challenges that we face as a nation to the ineffectiveness, lack of capacity and sometimes wickedness of our leaders but we neglect the fact that these leaders are essentially Nigerians and that there are minute ways in which we all contribute to the stunted progress of our country. One of such is the almost universal careless disposition to the respect for, and preservation of, human life.

Let me share one recent sad event with you. Some weeks ago, a man, possibly in his 60s left a construction site where he was a supervisor for his home in the Berger area of Lagos. He crossed the expressway and was suddenly hit by a careless bus driver. Immediately the incident happened, a witness said passengers came out of the bus, apparently unwilling to be found at the scene by law enforcement agents. The bus driver was said to have hurriedly packed the writhing victim into his bus saying to those who were watching that he would take the man to a medical facility.

No one asked questions about the specific medical facility he was taking the victim to, no one took down the registration number of his bus as he was said to have been an intercity driver. He was allowed to take the man away while every other person went about their businesses. Oh well, there was one concerned man, who was said to have found the wallet of the victim on the spot of the accident and called his family to alert them about what happened, where it happened and the decision of the driver to, all by himself, take the victim to the hospital.

Until well past midnight, the family combed hospitals from around Berger, the Accident and Emergency Unit at the 7up area of Lagos, where the victim would have received treatment, Magodo, Shangisha, Ketu and the entire vicinity without success. The search continued for the next two days and it would only be on the third day that the attention of the family was drawn to a dead body that had been dumped somewhere around Orile, tens of kilometres from the scene of the accident.

The family quickly rushed to the scene, unsure of what to meet, hoping against hope that their father would be found alive rather than dead. On arrival, it was the body of their otherwise bubbly father that they found. And even as they grieved over the untimely death of their patriarch, they found consolation in the retrieval of his corpse, days after a heartless driver chose self-preservation over the noble opportunity to save a life.

This raises question about the value we place on human life in this country. In a country where people thought more about the sanctity of life, the system would provide rapid response instruments that ensure people are taken care of. And where that is not available, he would have been taken to a nearby hospital under the supervision of witnesses. He possibly would be alive with his family today but here, he had no chance.

Gone are the days when Nigerians considered the preservation of life as a common duty. This is why some medical personnel will place priority on money over the prescription of their professional pledge to save lives. Stories abound of doctors refusing to attend to patients because they were unable to afford pittances to register at their hospitals. I actually once, walked into a situation in which a child just lost his life because hospital workers insisted that nothing would be done until his petty trader single mother registered the child.

There are instances where mothers and newborns lose their lives to nothing but lack of prompt intervention from medical personnel. To complicate matters, the bereaved get the most inhuman treatment from the same people who could have saved their loved ones. "Blood on their hands: Who will save the Nigerian Child from 'Killer' Doctors?" published by *The Cable,* paints a vivid picture of the inhuman conditions that patients are subjected to in hospitals in Nigeria. It told of the sequential loss of children in the Oncology Ward of the Lagos University Teaching Hospital (LUTH) as well as the apathetic, sometimes, coldhearted reactions of medical personnel to bereavements freshly induced by their own lackadaisical behaviour.

A particular man who was said to have gone on a violent rage after losing his newborn few hours after he was born premature got a really rough treatment from the hospital. *The Cable* reported that he was "detained by the security men, and the authorities subsequently threatened to charge him for assault. His family members wondered if assault was anything compared to negligence leading to preventable death." This man's wife was still said to be in some unconscious situation at another hospital. How can such a man remain sane?

This attitude is carried over by our leaders at all levels. This is why over sixteen years after return to democratic governance, Nigeria cannot boast of a community health insurance scheme from which the common man could benefit. Governors of the states would rather embark on medical trips abroad than contemplate state-of the-art facilities that would benefit their people and promote medical tourism. We are a nation where only our own lives and those of our family members matter to us. It is the same reason the medical facility which services the seat of power in Abuja would have provisions higher than that of all tertiary medical institutions in the country put together in this year's approved budget, yet Mr President receives medical treatment abroad.

Outside the dysfunction in our medical facilities, you will hear stories about kidnappings for ritual purposes, about communities where young girls are paid to bring forth babies who would only become objects of ritual sacrifices moments after their first breath.

There are also various internecine wars that the country has witnessed. Neighbouring communities killing each other, turning their fields into rivers of blood, sometimes over very trivial issues that dialogue should resolve.

That is not to talk of the over 20,000 lives that have been lost to the Boko Haram insurgency in the past seven years and the latest terrorist encroachment of herdsmen who have killed not less than 1,000 people in the past couple of months.

These people were killed in some of the grisliest manner yet, their killers still walk around unpunished. In instances like the recent attack on Nimbo community in Enugu state, law enforcement agents neglected to protect citizens despite intelligence reports of an impending attack. Yet, no one has been called to answer for the dereliction of duty that led to the death of tens of harmless Nigerians in this incident. So how do we deter other law enforcement agents from abandoning their duties in future?

Beyond government however, I think the average Nigerian should be a bit more concerned about the life of the other person. No matter where we find ourselves, we should ensure that no human being loses his or her life without a chance to fight for it, and each of us willing to facilitate that fight. I think this is a conventional requirement for civilisation, one classification that our country should otherwise eminently qualify for.

The PUNCH
19 May 2016

Memo to the Nigerian Political Godfather

If Nigerian politicians were to invest a fraction of the time and energy exerted on undoing one another in the genuine quest of developing the country, Nigeria would be far advanced. In the past couple of weeks, the people have become dazed by the dizzying pace at which politicians have crossed carpets from one party to the other. The other day, a former governor of Kano state, Mallam Ibraham Shekarau, capped up the ridiculous defections when he went back to the All Progressives Congress from the People's Democratic Party for the same reasons that he switched from the former to the latter four years ago. He made no shame of it at all as he addressed a press conference lamenting the failure of the PDP to protect his interest. None of it is ever about the people. It is only about the relevance and feathering of the nests of the political heavyweights. With Shekarau and the Uduaghans, Atikus, Sarakis and Kwankwasos were a multitude of political sheep following their shepherd where he leads, hardly any questions asked, and none answered.

When not jumping ship, politicians are busy playing the overlord. Insisting on who gets what and at what cost, enthroning and dethroning regardless of what such decisions might cost the country or its people. But the Nigerian politician forgets that power is transient and that the only time power makes sense in any enduring way is when it is deployed to the advantage of the people. And you seldom see that in Nigeria because power is absolute here. Those who hold it think of no one else but themselves. The arrogance of power and incessant victories over the years, have taken over the hearts of Nigerian politicians so they regard no one but themselves in the ever-increasing treachery that having their hands on the purse of the nation has become. Yet, there is no greater peril than the avarice and overconfidence that past triumphs bring and when it deals its cold hand, such consequences are usually fatal on the careers of the unwary.

In the book, *48 Laws of Power,* Robert Greene tells of the story of a young man known as Cyrus. Cyrus was a powerful young man who mobilised a huge army to depose his own grandfather as King of Medes in 559 BC. After this battle, Cyrus went on to become the King of Medea and Persia and began an expansionist drive of his kingdom to build a Persian empire. Victory followed victory for him and before long, he had defeated Croesus, ruler of Lydia, conquered the Ionian Islands and gone on to appropriate so many of the smaller kingdoms around him. Cyrus marched on and conquered Babylon after which he became known as Cyrus the Great, King of the World.

Having taken over Babylon and all its riches, Cyrus thought to expand on the east with a target on the half-barbaric tribe of the Massagetai, a vast realm on the Caspian Sea. Even though this race of warriors did not have any of the riches of Babylon, which he just conquered, Cyrus was obsessed with taking over this territory especially as he saw himself as the unconquerable king of the world.

In preparation for attack, Cyrus was said to have, in 529 BC, marched to a river which was the gateway to the Kingdom of Massagetai. As he set camp on the western bank of the river, he received a letter from the leader of the Massagetais, a female warrior known as Queen Tomyris. In the letter, Tomyris admonished the ambitious man of Persia in a very convivial way as follows: "King of Medes, I advise you to abandon your enterprise, for you cannot know if in the end, it will do you any good. Rule your own people and try to bear the sight of mine ruling mine."

However, she obviously knew that Cyrus at the time already crossed the lines of reason and like the dog destined to stray would not listen to the hunter's warning whistle, the aggressor would be too drunk on his own relevance to heed advice. So, she continued: "But of course, you will refuse my advice, as the last thing you wish for is to live in peace."

And she was right. Cyrus chose to go on with his expedition. Confident of her army's prowess, Tomyris offered to withdraw her troops from her own side of the river thereby allowing the attacking army to cross it without waters and fight her army on the eastern side. Cyrus agreed but rather than engage in a direct fight, he played a trick on the Massagetai army.

Privy to the deprivation suffered by the people he was marching on, Cyrus, after crossing the river prepared a large banquet, full of meat, delicacies and strong wine in the camp that he had set up. He then left the weakest links in his army on the camp and withdrew with the rest of the army.

A large Massagetai army soon attacked the camp, killing all the soldiers they encountered. After this, the victorious army got taken by their appetites and attacked the food and wine with the same enthusiasm with which they fought the soldiers on the Persian camp. But that was their undoing. They soon all fell asleep and became victims to the sword of the returning Persian Army. Spargapises, son of Queen Tomyris and a few of his soldiers, became prisoners of war while most of the army died in the battle.

On learning about this, the Queen penned another letter to Cyrus. "Now listen to me and I will advise you for your own good: Give me back my son and leave my country with your forces intact and be content with your triumph over a third part of the Massagetai. If you refuse, I swear by the sun, our master, to give you more blood than you can drink, for all your gluttony."

Again, Cyrus scoffed at the letter insisting that his conquest of Tomyris and her people must be total. While all of this was going on, the queen's son took his own life in lieu of the humiliation his continued imprisonment indicated and that inflamed the Queen. She immediately mobilised everyone and everything that was left of her army and, in a vengeful frenzy engaged Cyrus in a battle of no return. In time, she prevailed and rather than being caught alive, Cyrus killed himself. But the Queen was not satisfied, she searched for the corpse of the erstwhile king of the world. On finding it, she cut off his head and shoved it into a wineskin full of blood screaming: "Though I have conquered you and live…see now—I fulfil my threat: You have your fill of blood!" That act of unbridled ambition and selfish arrogance wrecked Cyrus and the empire that he strove to build.

Greene told this story to explicate the intoxicating influence of power, the sense of accomplishments that it brings to people who wield it and the unmitigated fall that accompanies the neglect to deploy power with discretion. How much you would wish that the Nigerian politician who feels he holds the world in the palm of his hands would learn a lesson or two from the transience and infallibility of it all.

As the country moves closer to the 2019 elections, powerful politicians in the country will sing the song of invincibility into their own ears. And when they do not, people around them would beat the drums for them. The greatest wisdom to borrow at moments like this, however, is to put the common good ahead of all personal interests. Used to running Nigeria's hundreds of million lives from their minuscule political parlours, the Nigerian politician will hardly see reason in succumbing to the will of the people; but the best dancer is not the one who dances all the time rather it is that who knows when the rhythm changes or stops entirely.

The PUNCH
13 September 2018

We Sure Need to Pray for Nigeria

The Nigerian intelligentsia, at least a sizeable number of them, are nauseated by religious Nigerians' penchant to pray about everything concerning the country. I have also noticed that they have allies in the diaspora.

The intelligentsia's posture is that the preponderance of Nigeria's problems is a direct result of bad leadership. Therefore, rather than sleep in churches, seeking divine intervention in our affairs, Nigerians should roll up their sleeves to get our government working by some more "practical" means.

I have heard many of those who preach this position cite attractive examples like how the Obamas and Camerons of this world are making impact without religious citizens. I have heard suggestions that when we pray about Nigeria, it should be restricted to the days of worship on Fridays and Sundays, and we should spend productive moments doing something "progressive". I have come to realise over the years that the word "progressive" means launching criticisms (constructive or otherwise) against the government, engaging in public protests against the ineffectiveness of government and on rare occasions, daring to join the political game to effect change from the inside out.

If ineptitude were a medical condition, we would gladly send our president and other government officials to a five-star medical facility in the United States of America or Germany or even in Saudi Arabia for a quick procedure that would turn them into highly skilled and performing leaders. But no medicine has yet to give us such luxury.

May be the best option is to vote for people better next time? That would be worth the try, but there would be no general elections for at least another 25 months in Nigeria. The implication is that we are stuck with this government for close to the next three years, and not even the impeachment of the president (if we were to contemplate that) would make our lot better.

Moreover, where are the better politicians? When Nigerians stop deceiving themselves, we will agree that not one of our political parties is giving the people a fairer deal. If you find any governor who stands out, I am convinced that it is because of his personal conviction to make impact rather than a political party interest in our welfare.

I am not saying that we do not have good people in politics; my point is that the Nigerian political climate makes it almost impossible for the good ones to have access to public office. It negates the interest of the operators of the political system – the godfathers who sit in their homes to administer our parties; those who play on Nigerians' emotions, selling piety they do not possess. When our political gladiators are not inept, they are selfish, inconsiderate and brutal.

If we take our focus away from leadership for just a bit, an objective appraisal of the Nigerian situation would show that we have more to worry about than the incapacities of our leaders. For instance, the state of the family unit. What about the communal values we used to know? What has happened to the sanctity of lives that we once held in esteem? It is in this same country that gangsters can march into a place of worship, kill people including women and children in cold blood and brag about it.

It is in this same country that people who are charged with ensuring that aircrafts are in safe condition sacrifice the lives of hundreds for some gratification. We live in a country where a father would surrender his child to ritualists for pecuniary gains. A country where a mother, entrusted with the divine responsibility of child rearing, will sell her baby without care if the infant will be slaughtered after purchase. A country where you serve the government for several years and become a communal disgrace if you did not amass wealth enough to last generations after you. A country where lives no longer mean anything. Imagine if one or all of the characters listed above emerged in government at once—and they do. This is why we are in this state.

So, where do we go from here? I believe we should continue to speak to God. I have read in my Bible that He interferes in the affairs of men. I also read somewhere in the Bible that God owns the hearts of kings and He turns them around like a water course (the way He wants). I remember that I read of how God humbled King Nebuchadnezzar for his pride; how he lost his sanity and lived like an animal for seven years. I remember how God dealt with King Pharaoh when he would not let the people of God go in peace, and I remember how King Herod was eaten alive by worms because "he did not give honour to God", which is the same thing every wicked leader would be guilty of.

And if a leader is inept or clueless, the God who gave wisdom to Solomon is the only one capable of performing a surgical operation that may change the nature of the unwise. That is for as long as we attribute the cause of our problems to leadership. However, the average Nigerian needs some deliverance from the spirit of self. We need a revival in our minds that I believe only sincere prayers can avail us. It is God who can affect the minds of those who kill innocent souls for sport. Only God can affect the minds of hundreds of thousands of Nigerians, who are waiting for the day they will get into government for no other reason than to get their hands on the national cake. Do not be deceived, God does such things.

I read the following story on a website called "#Just30Minutes" recently:

"In the 19th century, Korea was an isolated and primitive land riddled with fear and superstition. But in 1907, a small band of missionaries decided to redirect its course. Following news of the Welsh revival, they decided to come together and pray for Korea. They agreed to meet together to pray, daily, at noon. But at the end of one month, "nothing happened." One brother suggested the prayer meetings be discontinued. "Let us each pray at home as we find it convenient," he said. The others insisted they increased the time spent in prayer instead. So prayers continued, fervently, for another four months. Then a revival broke out. Church services here and there were interrupted by people weeping and confessing their sins. Multitudes flocked to the churches out of curiosity. Some came to mock, but fear laid hold of them, and they stayed to pray. Amongst the "curious" was a brigand chief, the leader of a band of robbers. He was convicted and converted. He went straight off to the magistrate and gave himself up. "You have no accuser" said the astonished official, "yet you accuse yourself! We have no law in Korea to meet your case." So, he dismissed him. By 1912 there were approximately 300,000 Korean church members in a total population of twelve million. A small band of praying Christians had changed a once primitive land for good. Korea rode on the crest of this revival, surviving Japanese domination, and civil war, to become one of the most orderly and prosperous places on earth".

Even almighty America has passed through this course more than once in its history. I remember reading that at a time in the USA, "bank robberies occurred daily. Street crime, rape and murder were rampant, and citizens were afraid to go out of their homes at night. Profanity was the worst imaginable, shocking in its filthiness". But in 1794, Pastor Isacc Backus, a Baptist Preacher called on ministers of the gospel in America to unite in prayer for the nation. People responded and before he realised it, a network of prayer meetings emerged across the country; some of them coordinated and prayed at the same time wherever they were. Gradually, there was a revival that reflected in every aspect of national life.

This is not to suggest that we should fold our arms and get lazy, waiting for God to do the basic things expected of us. It is an attempt to awaken us to the reality that the Divine could pierce the deep things that we do not understand about our nation, crown our own efforts and make everything work out for our good. That is if we call on Him.

I believe everyone who loves Nigeria should pray for the country and its leaders—I would like to think that they are the ones who really love Nigeria without motive. They do not call press conferences to score some populist goals; they do not do it to get a chance at a political ticket, and they are not doing it for fat support from the international community. Those who pray for Nigeria do so with the conviction that beyond the rot in our minds (both governor and governed), there is a God who is interested in the affairs of the country; a God who will look down from heaven and answer the prayers of His people. Those who bend their knees in prayers in the privacy of their rooms, or in public worship places to call on God, are working for us. If we cannot join them, please let us not run them down. They are working for a revival; a moral and spiritual revival that we all need to survive.

Therefore, "Men ought always to pray and not faint".

The PUNCH
3 September 2012

Boko Haram, Northern Leaders and the Conspiracy Of Silence

"...In keeping silent about evil, in burying it so deep within us that no sign of it appears on the surface, we are implanting it, and it will rise up a thousand-fold in the future. When we neither punish nor reproach evildoers, we are not simply protecting their trivial old age, we are thereby ripping the foundations of justice from beneath new generations." – Aleksandr Isayevich Solzhenitsyn

I will never understand how this Boko Haram phenomenon got this far. Sometimes when I read about their atrocities, I pinch myself to be sure that this is still the same Nigeria where I grew up. Things have really gone out of hand in this country.

Incredible things have started to happen here. One of them is the total lack of respect for the elderly. When I was growing up, no one would dare harm the elderly. One day we knew we would advance in age too, and we believed that anyone who wanted to grow old would not treat the elderly with disregard. This is the custom in the North, where religious, monarchical and patriarchal authority are almost incontestable, and elders are revered. But all that has evaporated before our eyes.

A few hours before I started writing this, Nigeria's one-time Minister of Petroleum, Dr Shettima Ali

Monguno, was kidnapped in Maiduguri, the Borno State capital. I found the news unbelievable and disheartening, a telling sign of how fast we are plunging into the abyss. Ali Monguno is an extremely old man of ninety-two, he was returning from Jumat service where he had gone to worship God. Those are two immutable reasons why no one should have contemplated snatching the man.

Things have so changed that we can barely recognise ourselves again. But maybe we needed to get here. For years now, Boko Haram elements have terminated the lives of thousands in a variety of violent ways—some were slaughtered, bombed, shot, or burnt alive. Sex or age did not matter. Men were killed; women were killed, and children. These killers discriminated against nobody.

Although statistics will likely show that more Christians and Southerners, especially people from the South Eastern part of the country have died in the hands of these godless human beings, there were times that they did not care about the tribe or faith of the people they killed. They killed in churches and mosques. They killed in restaurants and drinking joints. They killed in marketplaces and on the streets. It was like they were possessed by the demon of destruction. At the last count, not fewer than three thousand people have lost their lives in the hands of these misguided elements.

Yet, the elders and leaders of the Northern stock have not made one concerted effort to put an end to this unfortunate menace. We are talking about a North that produced the current second, third and fourth citizens of the country—the Vice President, the Senate President and Speaker of the House of Representatives. A Northern Nigeria that parades the likes of Sultan of Sokoto, Emir of Kano and Shehu of Bornu; the Emir of Zauzau and many heavy weight traditional cum religious leaders. We are talking about a region that produced former leaders like General Yakubu Gowon, Alhaji Shehu Shagari, General Muhammadu Buhari, General Ibrahim Babangida and General Abdulsalami Abubakar. A region with countless elder statesmen and politicians, and nineteen state governors, God knows how many intellectuals in various fields, federal cabinet ministers, chairmen of boards and government parastatals, local government chairmen etc. All these people, including the top shots in government, do nothing but passively call on government to put an end to the killings.

The failure of these respected leaders to intervene in the insecurity that has taken over the North East, parts of the North West and North Central of Nigeria has always bothered me. Not even attacks on the governor of Niger State, the Shehu of Bornu, Emir of Fika and the Emir of Kano triggered the patriotic alarm in these leaders. I have concluded that there must either be some conspiracy at work, or the North is not as united and homogeneous as we believed in those days. We were told about a few mafia groups that took decisions, and the North fell in line. The last few years have indicated that this either existed in the imagination of some people or the North is up to some grand conspiracy.

I remember the recent blackmail by the Northern elites of the president to consider amnesty for the militants. Despite how bitter that tasted in my mouth, I thought these leaders were at last standing up to the situation, but Abubakar Shekau, the leader of Boko Haram, rejected the offer. He boasted that it was the federal government that should seek amnesty from the group. That shocked me because it begged the question: did the people who canvassed for amnesty not talk to the intended beneficiaries before they started harassing government? Did they just assume that amnesty would work for Boko Haram faithfuls? Shouldn't these Northern elders, including governors, have unified to arrest the situation in the North all these years?

In my opinion, it is the failure of these leaders that has brought us to where we are now. Now, the chickens are coming home to roost. These criminals have moved from killing the common man to kidnapping high-class targets. Suddenly, no one has a hiding place—not the poor, the rich, the young and the old. We are at the mercy of these cheap crooks. Our leaders have failed us by their silence and unless they find their voices promptly, there will be dire consequences for our future.

I guess this is what Russian writer and historian mean in the quote above. These leaders have kept quiet for too long. Thank goodness that it is not too late to save us all from the doom that continuous silence and tacit approval of this evil portend. Now is the time for everyone who commands some respect in the North to speak up and save the country from this avoidable bloodletting; unless there is some subtle message that the carnage is meant to send. We all should remember that when fire gets out of hand, it can consume the man who lit it.

The PUNCH
8 May 2013

Codeine and a Nation Permanently on Opium

In more ways than one, last week's hurried outlawing of the importation, production and sale of cough medicines with the codeine component in Nigeria, shows the gross lack of competence among public office holders.

Lack of competence is not always due to incapacity; sometimes, it could be an unwillingness to act or a lack of concern for the impact on the common man. Public officers who prioritise self-preservation over the collective cannot relate until the unlikely prospect of that harm comes close to their homes. One other deeply painful thing about the knee-jerk reaction that culminated in the sealing of three pharmaceutical companies on Monday, is that it took the stinging report from the British Broadcasting Corporation (BBC) for the government to act. At least three Nigerian media outlets namely *The PUNCH* newspaper, Channels TV and TV Continental (TVC) have done extensive reports on the escalating abuse of drugs for an assortment of reasons especially amongst teenagers across the country, in the last five years.

Even the Senate, an arm of the federal government, just six months back, called national attention to the codeine burden borne by the entire nineteen states in the Northern part of the country. It estimated that about three million bottles of codeine are consumed daily in Kano and Jigawa States alone, and called for speedy attention from the authorities. But government people hardly paid attention or else, last week's ban and the subsequent massive investigation launched by the National Agency for Food and Drug Administration (NAFDAC), would have been executed and forgotten years back. Nigeria would have been saved the epidemic of the daily consumption of millions of bottles of codeine.

But even when public officials are alert enough to see the alarm raised by the local media and other citizens, they are too deep in survivalist deference and eye-service with appointed authorities to contemplate the situation. Sadly, these unconscientious public officials and many Nigerians do not seem to understand the jeopardy the country faces due to this lackadaisical attitude.

Now that the Federal Ministry of Health and its agencies are stirred from their slumber and ready to bare their fangs, you wonder how much they can do. How far are they willing to go? How many governors realise that to solve this problem demands a collaboration that is as dogged as it is deliberate? But we shall return to this point. Since there is no protocol on resolving any situation in Nigeria, NAFDAC, has in consonance with tradition, hit the sledge-hammer on the ant by shutting down pharmaceutical companies named in the expose like that would wipe out the scourge. But there are a couple of questions that the agency and its superintending ministry should answer:

Are they certain that Emzor, Peace Standard and Bioraj, all named in the BBC report, are the only pharmaceutical companies with codeine leakages in Nigeria?

Has the dragnet been extended to all other pharmaceutical companies and if so, how many more will be shut down when found guilty of dispensing this substance illegally?

Is there a way to track the operations and compliance of pharmaceutical companies whose business interest may supplant public good?

Even if all drug producing and importing companies in Nigeria were shut down or forced to comply with the established procedure for the sale of drugs laced with the addictive substance, what measures are in place to ensure that a country, which is unable to stop the smuggling of guns or rice, does not receive this banned substance through its legendary porous borders?

In case there is success with this attempt to ban codeine, a success for which there is no precedence in this country, what are the authorities doing to forestall chances of adulterations that could even be injurious?

It is doubtful that they have thought of these questions, which is another testimony of the tentative and absent-minded solutions that Nigeria proffers to issues.

However, assuming the action taken so far adequately addresses the challenges that codeine poses to Nigeria; does it address the reality that Nigerians found a means of getting high before the clampdown? Do the authorities also recognise that there are cheap alternatives in comparison to codeine? How would the interventions prevent youths from a reign of sniffs from gum and septic tanks; abuse of spirits, marijuana and many other cheap alternatives as a result of the ban on codeine? Addicted people do not come out of addiction because of the ban on substances; rather, they get free of the destructive habit through rehabilitation programmes that attend to the issues that precipitated their addiction.

Furthermore, workers at the factory that have been shut and those that may be shut in future will complicate the unemployment market. It will add to the social economic pressure that probably led some who succumbed to addiction in the first place.

No one in government is talking about tending the millions of young ones who are currently under influence, neither does government see the need to declare a national emergency to redeem millions that are captive to drugs and save others that are at the fringe of temptation.

Nigerian leaders currently held down by their own opium addiction—to get into office or retain what they currently hold in 2019—do not see the correlation between the insurgency and the highest rate of drug abusers present in the Northern part of Nigeria. Neither the government nor those who voted for them see the growing disenchantment of the youth, the crash of the family unit, increasing domestic homicidal incidents, hitherto unknown sexual appetites and behaviour, the wave of kidnapping and the insecurity in the country as evidences of the arrest of the minds of men and women by forces beyond them.

But it is no surprise. Nigerians are pathetically, a people, permanently on opium. When it is not of the religious type that makes people dogmatic and unquestioning in the face of contradictions, it is the political type where men have become the gods of men and women. The younger generation have only taken their indulgence a notch higher than that of their forebears. That is the way of nature, the successor is expected to be an improvement of his precursor, whether for good or bad. So, is there any hope that Nigerians can ever make the best of blessings of natural order by investing in her future?

The PUNCH
10 May 2018

No One Should Rejoice Over Those Defections

Far too many things break the heart about Nigeria, but two of them take the cake. One is the selfishness of the country's political elite and the other is the naivety of the citizenry.

In a sense, one is a corollary of the other, but like the egg and the chick, it is hard to tell which of these national misfortunes precedes the other. Someone may say misfortune seems an extreme word to employ in the circumstance but that is exactly what it is, at least as far as Nigeria's democratic growth is concerned. Unless there is a reversal of the lack of principles that govern politics and the docility of the people, democracy will crawl on its knee eternally—that is if the country remains. I will explain.

On Tuesday, fifty-two federal legislators took a step that every Nigerian, not drunk on the opium of self-delusion, should have seen coming since June 2015. The reaction (or lack of it) of President Muhammadu Buhari and the All Progressives Congress (APC) to the emergence of Senator Bukola Saraki and Honourable Yakubu Dogara as President of the Senate and Speaker of the House of Representatives respectively, and the failure of the party to put the matter behind it and seek unity on behalf of the country, put the first tear in the now totally shredded *babanriga* of the APC.

The Italian philosopher, strategist and proponent of the "end justifies the means", Niccolo Machiavelli, suggested over five centuries ago that there is no real affinity between morality and loyalty, but there is at least common sense. Politics is essentially about interests – the politician's, his party's and then the people's. All of this presupposes that like all human institutions, forgiveness is pivotal to the organic growth of political parties. But rather than that virtue to rule the hearts of gladiators in the APC; rather, the vice of arrogance is too pre-eminent.

What is more pathetic about the Nigerian politician is his inability to learn from the past. Hubris, which made the APC ignore the raging fire on its roof as evidence in the breakdown in the relationships of stalwarts in Kano, Kaduna, Benue, Bauchi and a bunch of other states in the country, was the tragic flaw that tore the otherwise secure umbrella of the Peoples Democratic Party from which the APC took power in 2015. So why do they not take cues from the past?

That is because of the sense of invincibility that power gives the Nigerian politician. Here, power is absolute, and when they possess it, they do not only deploy it to their own advantage, they also suppress any opposition. Therefore, Chairman of the APC, Adams Oshiomhole, with the boast about his clout in his party despite the defections, should take a moment to reflect on the implications of Tuesday's massive exodus on the nation's democratic growth.

What the APC and its leaders do not seem to understand is that apart from the promise to put Nigeria on the path of sustainable development, they owe Nigeria the duty of advancing democracy; something that the country would never attain as long as politicians change parties like call girls switch benefactors. So, pride and a shameless urge to satisfy the self, thereby neglecting the interest of the people, form the most discernible characteristics of the Nigerian politicians.

The other, if not the bigger part of the tragedy, is the refusal of Nigerians to be true citizens of their country. For instance, how many of the legislators, who announced a switch in party loyalties earlier this week sought the opinion of their constituents before taking this important decision? Democracy is said to be the government of the people, by the people, for the people. But here, the people do not matter to most politicians whether they represent the people, or they are elected to govern. They always claim to take decisions on behalf of the people, but whatever you claim to have done for the people, without the input of the people, cannot truly be for the people.

You cannot, however, exonerate Nigerians who have submitted their freedom to other mortals. If Nigerians are not pandering to the dictates of religious leaders who have bestowed *godship* unto themselves, they deify politicians, becoming unquestioning by themselves and violent in the resistance of the right of others to query those elected into office, thereby flouting a basic demand of democracy.

How conceivable is it, for instance, that star-struck Nigerians can never see anything wrong in the actions or inactions of political leaders? This tendency, harmless as it *seems,* invariably provides ammunitions for politicians to be laws unto themselves in total disregard for the people who elected them. Politicians now only need Nigerians during the elections. But even then, the people's desires are secondary since they are in control of the resources. The electorate has therefore unwittingly thrown its breakfast to the dogs.

Ultimately, Nigeria is the loser while the APC, like the cripple who hears with drums of war for one year but chooses to stay put until bullets hit his door, has itself to blame for allowing dissents to fester until the huge rebellion that we saw on Tuesday. Nigeria's democracy takes a weakling blow every time this happens. The fact that those who left the APC left for the same reason they left the Peoples Democratic Party in 2014 is a heartrending testimony of our political parties' inability to learn to entrench internal democracy, party discipline, planning and strategic mobilisation of the people as their power base.

It is also a worrisome indication of the instability that might become an inherent part of the country's politics. If Nigeria witnessed massive political realignments in 2015 as a result of the determination of politicians to secure their individual ambitions and settle political scores, and the same thing happened now that the country is moving towards another general election, what is the guarantee that this perfidy would not occur in 2023, thereby becoming a permanent feature of Nigerian politics?

When it ran in the 2015 elections, the APC had just about five pillars of power, yet it has not known one day of peace since it took over power that same year. To call meetings of the National Executive Council has been herculean for the party, not to speak of constituting a board of trustees. If the APC with those relatively few interests failed to appreciate the collegiate character of party politics in an emerging democracy these three years, how would the congregation of embittered people coming together at the moment not turn Nigeria into a political war field post 2019, if they are able to win the election?

Therefore no one, not the defectors, not the PDP, which appears to be the greatest beneficiary of the civilian coup that occurred this week, nor their supporters should rejoice just yet. If this event ends as another power-grabbing initiative, this coalition, in another four years will be at the juncture that the APC currently finds itself. Of course, there is also the frightening prospects of destabilising the country and even tearing it apart. Political parties should provide rallying points for unity with members from across all nationalities.

What Nigerian political parties need to do currently is identify a common ideology that bind them together, grow internal democracy and give power back to the people. That not done, those who are rejoicing today, will be at the receiving end tomorrow and they will leave Nigeria, this huge country with enormous potential utterly unaccomplished. It is a bad dream that should never come to pass truly, but only a commitment to selfless work by the leader and led, will terminate that nightmare and change Nigeria for the better.

The PUNCH
26 July 2018

Acknowledgements

My gratitude:
To the Father of all light for His mercies that endure for ever
To my parents who taught me to love people
To Nkem, Tishe, Temi and Timi for their devotion and prayers
To my siblings whose prayers avail much
To all my friends, who I cannot begin to mention
To Adeola Ibrahim, brother and friend for his tireless support
To Mr Ademola Osinubi for another opportunity at *The PUNCH*
To Simon Kolawole for *The Cable* and much more
To Joseph Adeyeye for supporting a brother
To Joel Nwokoema for the good job which encourages
To Emeka Madunagu, for my very foundation
To Jonin Solt Ejemba who first sorted the articles
To Vannesa Obioha who did the first reading
And to Anwuli Ojogwu, my editor without who, you will not be holding this book.
May the good Lord bless you all.

About the Author

Niran Adedokun is a public relations practitioner, lawyer and writer. He is the author of *Ladies Calling the Shots*, a profile of seventeen top female film and television directors in Nigeria, released in 2017. Adedokun is also a columnist with *The PUNCH* and TheCable.ng newspapers.

The Danfo Driver in All of Us and Other Essays, a compilation of his reflections on national issues, published over a period of five years, is his second book.